Beyond Connectivity: Exploring Privacy Concerns in South Africa's Use of the Internet of Things

Chopra

Table of Contents

1. Introduction

The number of internet of things (IoT) devices and services continues to mushroom, with their presence in people's lives ever-present, considering that a smartphone is considered an IoT device (Aleisa & Renaud, 2017b). Worldwide shipments of smart wearables have increased by almost 95% between 2018 and 2019 (Llamas, Ubrani, & Shirer, 2019). Privacy is a big concern and obstacle for the penetration of IoT services, in a period in which privacy leakages are on the rise (Kim, Park, Park & Ahn, 2019). Research suggests that society value their privacy (Buchwald, Letner, Urbach & von Entreß-Fürsteneck, 2017), which refers to an individual being able to control information about himself/herself (Crossler & Bélanger, 2017; Hossain & Prybutok, 2008). However, individuals often act to the contrary (Williams, Nurse & Creese, 2017). This phenomenon is referred to as the privacy paradox (Barth, de Jong, Junger, Hartel & Roppelt, 2019). Williams (2018) goes on to state that individuals engage in activities that endanger their privacy, such as the use of social media and IoT (Kim, et al., 2019). An on-going trend relates to Individuals often failing to read and adhere to policies, check permissions or protecting their information (Williams, 2018), in an environment where everything is connected, it is inevitable that private information will increasingly become available to IoT service providers and increases the risk of leakage (Kim et al., 2019).

The purpose of this research is to understand the cause of the privacy paradox in South Africa (SA) in the use of IoT, by identifying the factors that influence the willingness to disclose personal information in the use of IoT within SA. Previous research confirms that the privacy paradox exists in social media (Gross & Acquisti, 2005; Koklakis, 2015), but the question still remains: what are the factors that cause the privacy paradox in the use of IoT? In other words, why do people disclose their personal information, although they are concerned about their data? (Beuker, 2016). This study aims to contribute to those gaps in research, where research is still in its infancy in the context of IoT (Williams, 2018). The main facet of IoT is not only about connectivity but rather the pervasive collection and sharing of data for the purpose of enabling autonomous services and actions (Lopez, Rios, Bao, & Wang, 2017). Therefore, the dominant criticism of IoT is the possibility of creating a world where individuals' privacy is constantly being infringed upon, subsequently giving rise to a "surveillance society" (Novotny,

Dávid, & Csáfor, 2015); making privacy an important topic within research and industry (Wu, Zhang, Cui & Wang, 2018).

A possible explanation of why individuals disclose their personal information relates to the Privacy Calculus (Wang, Duong & Chen, 2016). The theoretical underpinnings of the privacy calculus explain a rational decision-making process in which individuals set up a benefit-risk analysis of a situation to decide whether or not to disclose information (Wang, Duong & Chen, 2016), where possible benefits could outweigh the potential risks i.e. loss of privacy (Krasnova, Kolesnikova & Guenther, 2009). This research incorporates the privacy calculus as a theoretical foundation in an attempt to understand the cause of the privacy paradox in the use of IoT. "IoT service providers realise that consumers want more benefits despite their concerns about privacy. There is even a tendency to lower the weight on perceived privacy risks and pursue perceived benefits" (Kim et al., 2019, p. 1).

However, it is assumed that there are more factors than perceived risks and perceived benefits that influence the privacy paradox (Beuker, 2016). Therefore, after analysing previous literature which will be elaborated on in further sections, this study localised the following factors as possible key tenants in relation to willingness to disclose personal information; 1. *information sensitivity* – information which is personally identifiable or regarded as critical information with varying degrees of associated risk (Schomakers, Lidynia, Müllmann & Ziefle, 2019), 2. *privacy concerns* – concern for privacy is subjective as different people associate different levels of risk to their information (Buchanan, Paine, Joinson & Reips, 2007), 3. *social influence* – refers to the social influence of one user/group of users on another, which has become an important factor in modern information and service industries (Peng, Yang, Cao, Yu & Xie, 2017), 4. *privacy knowledge* – knowledge of how much users actually understand about the risks and threats associated to their privacy (Gabriele & Chiasson, 2020), alongside 5. *perceived benefits* and 6. *perceived privacy risks*.

1.1. Research Problem

With the accelerated growth in online activities, devices and platforms; there has subsequently been an equal rise in the amount of personal information being submitted online to use various services and products (Salahuddin & Gow, 2016). Today, the prevalence of IoT is a privacy risk because the technology has become ubiquitous and continuously pursuing data collection (Williams, 2018). Conti et al. (2018) agreed, stating that many IoT objects are collecting and processing private information to achieve autonomous services and connections, inherently making these objects rich sources of information for malicious attackers to exploit. That being said, research indicates that IoT users expect the confidentiality of their personal information be kept intact (Kim et al., 2019), even though individuals have become accustomed to disclosing and sharing personal information without hesitation (Barth et al., 2019). Revealing personal data has simply become a part of everyday life (Castro & Bettencourt, 2017), in which individuals are encouraged through benefits such as personalisation but discouraged by privacy concern (Lai, Liang & Hui, 2018). The benefits and proposed ease of living are undeniable, however, the rise in unprecedented loss of privacy may be a subsequent cost/risk (Lopez et al., 2017).

Therefore, despite the appeal of IoT, there is a concern pertaining to potential threats to individuals' privacy in the use of devices and applications (Hallam & Zanella, 2016; Williams et al., 2017). Paradoxically the growing concern has not inhibited people from treating their privacy as a commodity (Buchwald et al., 2017), and continuously enriching IoT objects despite their concern (Conti et al., 2018), knowingly or unknowingly (Lopez et al., 2017; von Entreß-Fürsteneck, Buchwald, & Urbach, 2019). Most research orientated around the privacy paradox emphasises its existence and studies positioned on explaining the cause of the actual paradox have not been fully realised (Han, Shen, Zhou, Xu, Miao, & Qi, 2019). Figure 1 depicts the growing importance and prevalence of privacy orientated research with respect to IoT within the last decade (Román-Castro, López, & Gritzalis, 2018, p.19), although very few have focused on the privacy paradox (Williams, et al., 2017).

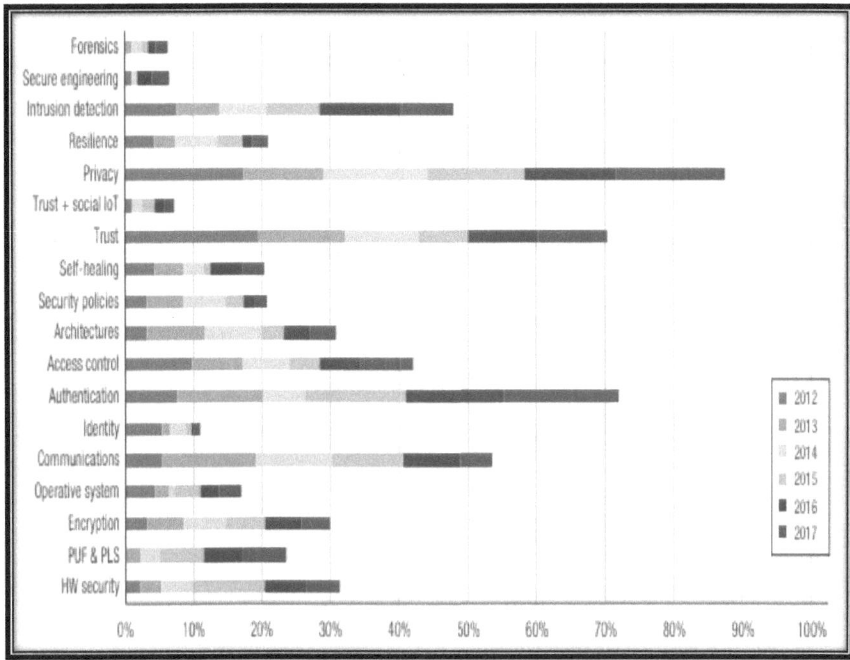

Figure 1. Evolution of the importance of every IoT security area. (Román-Castro, López, & Gritzalis, 2018, p.19).

Lopez et al. (2017) explains that most studies consider privacy as a part of a broader security analysis, rather than recognising privacy as a problem in its own right, while research addressing whether that paradox exists, has predominately focused on areas within Northern America (NA) and the United Kingdom (UK). Therefore, it is important to evaluate whether the paradox exists and the reasons for its existence in SA as perceptions vary in different cultures (Williams, 2018). Research related to privacy awareness in respect to information disclosure, has yet to mature (von Entreß-Fürsteneck, Buchwald, & Urbach, 2019), countries within Africa are associated with insufficient levels of privacy awareness and education (Kritzinger, 2017). Ensuring privacy awareness and a culture orientated around security in SA is problematic because of economic dispensation, knowledge, access to information and technology and various languages used within the country (Kritzinger, 2017).

1.2.   Purpose of the Study

This study aims to understand the cause of the privacy paradox in the use of IoT in SA, through identifying key factors that influence individuals' willingness to disclose personal information. Below are the research objectives:

1.2.1. Research Questions

Below are the research questions incorporated within this study. By answering these questions, this research attempts to determine what are the key influencing factors that lead individuals to disclose personal information in the use IoT in SA?

Main Research Question:

What are the key influencing factors that impact an individual's willingness to disclose personal information in the use of IoT in SA?

Sub-Research Questions:

1.2.1.1.   How does the sensitivity of the information being requested by IoT influence individuals' intention to disclose their personal information in the use of IoT?

1.2.1.2.   How does privacy concern influence individuals' intention to disclose their personal information in the use of IoT?

1.2.1.3.   How does the calculus of perceived benefits influence individuals' intention to disclose their personal information in the use of IoT?

1.2.1.4.   How does the calculus of perceived risk influence individuals' intention to disclose their personal information in the use of IoT?

1.2.1.5.   How does privacy knowledge influence individuals' intention to disclose their personal information in the use of IoT?

1.2.1.6.   How does social influence affect individuals' intention to disclose their personal information in the use of IoT?

1.2.1.7.   How would individuals that use IoT in SA react if their information is at risk of being compromised?

1.2.2. Research Objectives

Main Research Objective:

Ascertain what are the key influencing factors that lead individuals to disclose personal information in the use IoT in SA?

1.2.2.1. Determine whether information sensitivity influences individuals' intention to disclose their personal information in the use of IoT.

1.2.2.2. Evaluate whether privacy concern influences individuals' intention to disclose their personal information in the use of IoT.

1.2.2.3. Critically assess how the calculus of perceived benefits influence individuals' intention to disclose their personal information in the use of IoT.

1.2.2.4. Critically assess how the calculus of perceived risk influence individuals' intention to disclose their personal information in the use of IoT.

1.2.2.5. Determine how privacy knowledge influence individuals' intention to disclose their personal information in the use of IoT.

1.2.2.6. Examine how individuals' social relationships affects intentions to disclose their personal information in the use of IoT.

1.2.2.7. Determine whether individuals are more likely to exhibit self-withdrawal or disclosure tendencies, if their privacy is at risk.

1.3.   Research Method

This research takes on an objective ontological view, with the underlying epistemological stance being positivistic as the aim of this study is to objectively understand the cause of the privacy paradox within the context of IoT by identifying factors that influence information disclosure in SA. This research incorporates a deductive approach, employing the use of a conceptual model which was constructed from a combination of studies orientated around privacy, the privacy calculus and the privacy paradox. Data for this research was collected using the quantitative research approach, through the use of an anonymous online questionnaire (Bhattacherjee, 2012; Saunders, Lewis, & Thornhill, 2009). The targeted population was narrowed down to the general public residing within SA that make use of IoT devices and/or services. The privacy paradox should not be associated as a symptom of only young people but rather a process that concerns all ages (Kokolakis, 2017). Therefore, samples should be as representative as possible, which supports the approach of this study focusing on the general public.

1.4.1. This research assumes that the majority of respondents are not experts in the field of IoT, therefore they will have a limited understanding of IoT, and the potential risks involved.

1.4.2. This research assumes that when people are worried about their privacy, they are careful about disclosing their personal information (Beuker, 2016).

1.4.3. This research assumes that the following IoT technologies are used by the general public include but are not limited to wearables, smart TVs, fitness bands, smart appliances, laptops, smartphones and tablets etc. (Sinha, 2017; Williams et al., 2017).

1.4.4. This study focused on individuals in SA, therefore, individuals living outside of SA will be excluded. The targeted population incorporates the general public that make use of IoT devices and/or services, to solicit responses from various individuals, such as non-experts, experts, non-professionals as well as professionals (Williams et al., 2017).

1.4.5. Through the adoption of a survey strategy and the combination of a questionnaire, there is a limit to the number of questions that can be asked (Saunders et al., 2009). While a survey strategy is able to elicit information about factors relating to attitudes and perceptions, which is difficult to measure through a more observational approach, the strategy merely provides estimates rather than exact measurements (Glasow, 2005).

1.5.   Significance of Study

The results from the research will assist in identifying factors that influence individuals information disclosure in the use of IoT and providing an illustration of the current privacy climate within SA, which may result in the improvement of privacy standards of the actual devices and the potential improvement of privacy awareness within SA (Castro & Bettencourt, 2017; Williams et al., 2017; Zheng, Chetty & Feamster, 2018). This study can provide further guidance on the theoretical factors that cause the privacy paradox, particularly within the context of the IoT.

1.6.   Ethics and Ethical Considerations

All participants in this study were ensured that their responses were/always will be treated with anonymity, although demographical information such as age and gender were collected and used in an attempt to accomplish stipulated research objectives. This research has gone through the ethical clearance process overseen by the UCT Ethics committee. Further ethics and ethical considerations are detailed in 3.5.

1.7.   Structure of book

The following chapter focuses on the literature review, detailing the literature findings, the formulation of the hypotheses which was tested to answer the research questions, theoretical understandings and the constructed conceptual model used within this study. Chapter 3 is orientated around the research design and methodology process, illustrating what research and data collection practices were followed in this study. Chapter 4 consists of the data analysis and findings sections, providing an in-depth analysis of the data gathered during the data collection phase. Chapter 5 consists of the summary, discussion and recommendation sections, as well the concluding remarks related to the study.

2. Literature Review

2.1. Introduction

Over the past fifteen years technology has changed human interaction and environments (Aljallad, Guo, Chouhan, LaPerriere, Kropczynski, Wisnewski, & Lipford, 2019). Through the high level of heterogeneity, coupled with the intensive push IoT technologies are currently receiving, there is an expectancy that privacy concerns will be magnified (Sicari et al., 2015). Aljallad et al. (2019) emphasises this by explaining that because of the advancement of technology, personal information has never been as exposed nor as accessible as it is today, a trend which is expected to continue as data collection and new technologies become more apparent. Privacy behaviour is highly contextual (Morando, Iemma, & Raiteri, 2014), Kokolakis (2017) stated that because of this, it cannot be expected that individuals will demonstrate the exact same behaviour in different contexts. One individual may readily disclose their information over a platform or device, while another may oppose access in its entirety, privacy perceptions can differ greatly due to culture or location (Williams, 2018).

Williams (2018) states that because of the ubiquitous nature of smart devices and the potential risk they pose, it is subsequently important to support users in making informed decisions and realigning behaviour with privacy concerns. Situations involving the compromise of individuals' personal information continues to rise as Internet adoption increases; while new security vulnerabilities are created using mobile Internet access (Choudhury, Basak & Guha, 2013). Individuals are able to spend longer periods of time online, larger amounts of data are now being outsourced to third-party organisations, which subsequently creates increased avenues of risk when securing information privacy (Choudhury et al., 2013), which is exacerbated through IoT technologies (Weber, 2015; Williams, 2018). The decreasing cost of storing digital data has assisted in capturing, analysing and retaining increasing amounts of individuals' information (Carignani & Gemmo, 2018), although new methods of data collection in IoT has brought about new privacy challenges (Naeini et al., 2017). Some of these challenges include; enabling individuals to be able to control, customise and choose the data that they share, while ensuring that privacy and security is kept intact and that the collected data is used as its stated purpose (Naeini et al., 2017).

Individuals may generally decide not to disclose information that would affect the security of their data (Adelmeyer, Meier, & Frank Teuteberg, 2019). The above notion would be considered logical behaviour, although the progression of technology, data collection methods and human behaviour contradicts it and subsequently many individuals experience privacy issues such as targeted marketing, as well as security problems surrounding identity theft (Crossler & Belanger, 2017). Crossler and Belanger (2017) continue that although privacy remains a concern, the vast amounts of personal information collected by organisations as well as third parties can often occur without individuals being aware. Other considerations to take into account relate to the type of data being requested (information valuation) (Prince, 2018), perceived benefits (Wang et al., 2016), potential risks (Beuker, 2016), privacy knowledge/awareness (Macada & Luciano, 2010), Social influence (Mendel & Toch, 2017) and self-withdrawal (Dienlin & Metzger, 2016).

The purpose of this literature review was to assist in contextualising several concepts relating to the research topic through the analysis of previous literature. The following sections depict IoT in relation to information sensitivity, privacy concern, the privacy calculus, perceived benefits, perceived risks, social influence, self-withdrawal and privacy knowledge. This section of the study outlines and details the fundamental aspects related to the research topic to assist in answering the research questions.

2.2. Search Methodology

The search methodology was guided by the principles used by Garrido, Sey, Hart and Santana (2012), which were as follows:

- **Resources for executing the research**: The primary database used within this study included Google Scholar, through the progression of the research process, the research included UCT Libraries database and other databases such as; EBSCOHost, Emerald and ScienceDirect.
- **Type of literature**: The analysis incorporated data from relevant academic papers, peer-reviewed journals, articles and conference papers.
- **Publication date**: The search was filtered through the use of keywords and specific time periods to isolate and include research that was mainly cited between 2013 to 2020, with

the inclusion of a few older publications. During the mentioned period there was an increase in studies related to privacy (Román-Castro, López, & Gritzalis, 2018).

- **Language**: The search within this study was limited to English language texts because the majority of academic research is written in English (Garrido, Sey, Hart & Santana, 2012).
- **Key search terms**: Internet of Things (IoT); information privacy; information disclosure; privacy behaviours; privacy calculus; perceived benefits; perceived risks; privacy paradox; information sensitivity; social influence; self-withdrawal.

2.3.   Background Discussion

The IoT is defined "as an invisible network of networks, which collects and stores data, controls and interacts with people, and with physical and virtual things" (Attié & Meyer-Waarden, 2018, p.21), through the use of wireless connections to send data collected by sensors attached to those objects (Conti, Dehghantanha, Franke, & Watson, 2018; Zhou, Cao, Dong, & Vasilakos, 2017). IoT has been acknowledged as one of the most innovative forms of technology since the computer, because of the influence it can have on multiple sectors of physical and virtual environments (Henze et al., 2016; Hsu & Lin, 2016; Lopez et al., 2017; Sinha, 2017). IoT devices vary in form and purpose, from sensors that individuals carry on their wrists to vehicles, home appliances and smartphones (Naeini et al., 2017; Ponciano, Barbosa, Brasileiro, Brito & Andrade, 2017; Sinha, 2017). "While these devices bring about new services, increase convenience, and improve efficiency, they also bring privacy and security risks" (Naeini et al., 2017, p. 399). The most common forms of IoT used by individuals include smartphones and smartphone applications coupled with smart bands or smart watches used to monitor health and provide quick access to online services (Hallam & Zanella, 2016), as well as smart TVs, smart cars, lights and home appliances (Aleisa & Renaud, 2017b; Sinha, 2017).

The growth of IoT is expected to continue, by 2020 the number of connected devices is estimated to reach 50 billion (Attié & Meyer-Waarden, 2018; Irshad, 2016). Statista (2019a) reported that between 2013 and 2018 spending on IoT in the retail sector in SA increased from $27.9 million to an estimated $60 million, highlighting the technologies growing influence in the country from a consumer perspective. As IoT grows in importance; concerns regarding privacy, security, and reliability have become more relevant issues (Knowles, Beck,

Finney, Devine & Lindley, 2019). In a period where people nonchalantly accept terms and conditions of devices and applications, the compromise of information is on the rise because people are no longer aware of the extent to which their information can be accessed (von Entreß-Fürsteneck, Buchwald, & Urbach, 2019). In combination with the rapid growth of IoT, which has extended the internet to distributed environment; ensuring privacy is kept intact has become problematic (Witti & Konstantas, 2019).

Contrastingly Blythe and Johnson (2018) emphasise that because of potential privacy and security concerns, IoT adoption can subsequently stagnate, although adoption estimations illustrate a different view (Da Xu, He, & Li, 2014; Irshad, 2016). The data collected by IoT technologies has often been considered innocuous by individuals, while individuals tend to believe that they own the data produced by their IoT devices and often do not fully understand how the data is analysed or stored and for what purposes (Chen, Bovornkeeratiroj, Irwin & Shenoy, 2018). IoT technologies can expose individuals to privacy attacks, particularly related to sensor data collected, which can indirectly reveal sensitive data, such as an individual's activities and habits (Blythe & Johnson, 2018; Chen et al., 2018). Paradoxically users can experience greater benefits through providing more personal information (Kim et al., 2019). Despite the anxieties expressed around privacy vulnerabilities, people continue to use technologies that require personal information (Marwick & Hargittai, 2018).

2.4.   Privacy

Privacy in the context of this study is considered to be the concern of "what information an individual reveals about him/herself or his/her associations to others, and under what conditions and safeguards" (Caron et al., 2016, p. 6). This definition refers to what information people can keep to themselves without being forced or coerced into revealing to others (Aleisa & Renaud, 2017a). Privacy preferences are highly contextual and subjective (Williams et al., 2017; Wu et al., 2018), where individuals may value privacy in certain instances over others (Williams et al., 2017). Men and women have been found to display different levels of online privacy, female internet users have been found to be more concerned about online privacy violations, as well as perceive more information sharing-related risks than males do (Beldad & Hegner, 2017). Demographic differences (age, gender and education) influence the degree of general privacy concerns, where individuals who were less likely to be concerned about privacy were more likely to be young, male and less educated (Xu, Teo, Tan & Agarwal, 2012).

While many individuals have difficulties of actually managing their privacy over various platforms, leading some to avoid protecting themselves entirely (Wu et al., 2018). Protecting one's privacy when using IoT devices is a complex and difficult task, "the number of attack vectors available to malicious attackers might become staggering, as global connectivity ("access anyone") and accessibility ("access anyhow, anytime") are key tenets of the IoT" (Roman, Zhou & Lopez, 2013, p.2270). Individuals are generally hesitant to disclose personal information due to worries of their information being inappropriately collected and accessed by third parties (Wu et al., 2018). However, in the current technological climate, over-disclosure of personal information has become a normal practice within society (Choi, Park & Jung, 2018).

Two of the most common forms of crimes against personal information are **Identity theft** and **phishing**, in which identify theft is defined as the illegal use of an individual's personal information for fraudulent activities (Lindberg, 2011), while phishing is defined as the act of retrieving an individual's personal information by pretending to be a trustworthy third party (Hedayati, 2012). Currently phishing attacks are extremely prominent within SA, the 2019 *State of Email Security report* by Mimecast reported that 88% of their respondents (organisations within the country) confirmed that they had experienced a phishing attack since 2018 (BusinessTech, 2019). In line with the above, the occurrence of identity theft and phishing have gained momentum since the inception of e-commerce platforms, in which individuals supply their personal information in pursuit of some form of benefit (Kumar, 2012), difficulty comprehending how their technology works, or lack of attentiveness towards privacy and security (Dong, Clark & Jacob, 2010).

The threats that can affect an IoT device are growing, consisting of targeted diverse communication channels, physical threats, denial of service (DDoS), identity fabrication and human error (Choudhury et al., 2013; Roman, Zhou & Lopez, 2013; Sartain, 2015; Whitman & Mattord, 2013). The growing concern relating to IoT is the Mirai Botnet, for several hours in

2016 Twitter, Netflix and Reddit became unusable across Europe and the United States, where IoT devices were used as bots rather than more conventional hosts (Jerkin, 2017). "By compromising large numbers of IoT devices, the Mirai botmaster was able to generate massive amounts of attack traffic from legitimate network hosts" (Jerkin, 2017, p. 2). Bertino and Islam (2017) place emphasis on the need for more privacy-averse users, as IoT systems will continue to be susceptible to attacks because many devices do not have well-defined perimeters, which continuously change due to the mobility aspects of the devices.

2.5. Privacy Paradox

The privacy paradox is regarded as the central topic for this research, which refers to the disparity between the unexpected behaviour by people who are concerned about their privacy, but nevertheless disclose personal information (Beuker, 2016; Brown, 2001; Carignani & Gemmo, 2018). Personalised recommendation systems have played a big role in the increase of personal information being revealed by individuals (Anand & Mobasher 2003). Literature continuously highlights that people are the most significant contributors in the event of a security breach (Sillaber, & Breu, 2015; Ifinedo, 2012). People are associated to be the "weakest link" in information security, illustrating that user behaviour can be unpredictable, which can subsequently create unexpected scenarios (Belanger & Xu, 2015; Ifinedo, 2012). Williams (2018) states that there is a high chance that people do not often take action to protect their data, often failing to read policies or check access permissions, despite their concern for their privacy which emphasises the aforementioned disparity between claimed concern and actual behaviour. This view has been tested and reaffirmed in previous research (Norberg, Horne, & Horne, 2007; Sutanto, Palmen, & Phang, 2013; Xu, Luo, Carroll, & Rosson; 2011).

Brown (2001) was the first to bring up that a paradox existed through the author's qualitative research involving loyalty cards, in which even respondents that exhibited privacy concern were open to disclosing their personal information (Williams, 2018). The phenomenon had gained momentum and Norberg et al. (2007) work illustrated how immense the disparity was between concern and action. Their research depicted that over a short period of time individuals that claimed to be concerned about their privacy, eventually disclosed their personal information in an attempt to gain some form of benefit (Norberg et al, 2007). Most research on the privacy paradox mainly focused on theoretical discussions, only emphasising its existence and studies on explaining the cause of the paradox is still in its infancy (Han et al., 2019), particularly in the field of IoT (Williams, 2018). Beuker (2016) documented the privacy paradox through a comparison between Dutch and German respondents using social networking services (SNS), the aim of the research was to identity the reason the paradox existed. More recently, Williams (2018) has looked into how the paradox fits in with IoT as the phenomenon had previously been orientated around social media and with the current technological landscape incorporating these small nodes, his research was well poised to provide new understandings within the research paradigm. This research has extrapolated several facets from the latter two studies.

As technology improves, research around the paradox and information privacy grows in importance (Williams, 2018). Securing mobile devices becomes essential in a climate where they are being used on a daily basis, although on average only 10% of every 86 million mobile devices are considered to be "secure" (Beyer, 2014). This being said, information disclosure continues to grow through the use IoT (Williams, 2018), often due to individuals not understanding potential risks in doing so (Steijn & Vedder, 2015). Crossler and Belanger (2017) emphasise that there is a concern around how privacy is being ensured to individuals when disclosing personal information.

This research incorporates the privacy calculus as a theoretical foundation in an attempt to understand the cause of the privacy paradox in the use of IoT. The privacy calculus has previously been used to analyse privacy perceptions and behaviours of individuals (Jiang et al., 2013; Krasnova et al., 2010; Wang et al., 2016). The privacy calculus is a function that illustrates how individuals decide whether to disclose information based on a calculation from disclosure needs and privacy concerns, involving a benefits-risk trade-off (Jiang et al., 2013; Krasnova et al., 2010). Min and Kim (2015) define the privacy calculus as a process where individuals assess potential consequences of a present choice through weighing potential benefits against risks of divulging some degree of their privacy. Wang et al. (2016) explain that there are two main drivers for an individual's intention to disclose, **perceived benefits** and **perceived risks**. According to Anand and Mobasher (2003), perceived benefits increases individuals' intentions to disclose their personal information, while potential privacy risks inhibit over disclosure, restricting the amount of information an individual is willing to reveal. Therefore, when perceived benefits outweigh perceived risks, an individual is more likely to disclose personal information (Beuker, 2016). The above two drivers (perceived benefits and perceived risks) are important in the privacy calculus calculation because the calculation itself is only valid if individuals' assessment of potential benefits and risks incurred are based on a comprehensive understanding of those variables (Correia & Compeau, 2017; Hajli & Lin, 2016).

"The theoretical foundations of self-disclosure go back to Social Exchange theory, which posits that interpersonal relationships are based on a subjective evaluation of benefits and costs" (Krasnova et al., 2010, p.110). Subsequently this has formed the basis of the privacy calculus theory and therefore, expresses the notion that privacy loss is simply the price individuals may have to pay to receive benefits of services, whereby benefits of a relationship, such as trust building, mutual empathy and reciprocation, often outweigh the risks associated with increased vulnerability (Krasnova et al., 2010). Although, Krasnova et al., (2010) argue that other intangible benefits such as enjoyment, self-presentation; maintaining social ties, may all contribute to the act of self-disclosure. In the case of mobile applications and social media platforms, Zafeiropoulou, Millard, Webber and O'Hara (2013) draw upon the Structuration Theory, the authors put forward the notion that a privacy decision forms part of a structuration process, whereby individuals are not considered as entirely free agents when making a decision but are instead influenced by contextual factors, such as social norms and trust in an application (Kokolakis, 2017).

The privacy calculus has its limitations, because it is applied in scenarios where individuals are assumed to act in a rational manner (Beuker, 2016). Although research has progressed over time and the role of heuristics and biases have grown, while behavioural economics posits the increasing influence of other factors in a decision-making process (Williams, 2018). Williams (2018), goes on to explain that a lack of knowledge results in individuals overestimating potential benefits while risks cannot be accurately perceived. Therefore, this study incorporates additional factors.

2.7.   Context of Study within South Africa

The potential risk involved in IoT, refers to unauthorised use and misuse of individuals' personal data, which subsequently increases privacy concern (Libaque-Saenz, Chang, Kim, Park & Rho, 2016). A breach of an individual's privacy relates to the disclosure of their information without their consent, where the disclosure can be either intentional or unintentional (Saeri, Ogilvie, Macchia, Smith, & Louis, 2014). Research indicates that a paradox occurs where individuals are increasingly being put in a trade-off situation, where a decision occurs to disclose their personal information for receiving some benefit (Crossler & Bélanger, 2017; Jiang, Heng & Choi, 2013; Xu et al., 2011). In these cases, expected benefits tend to be overestimated (Gómez-Barroso, Feijóo & Martínez-Martínez, 2018). The 'digital population' of SA has increased dramatically over the last few years, in January 2019 SA had an estimated 31.18 million internet users, figure 2 depicts; 28.99 million were mobile internet users (Statista, 2019b).

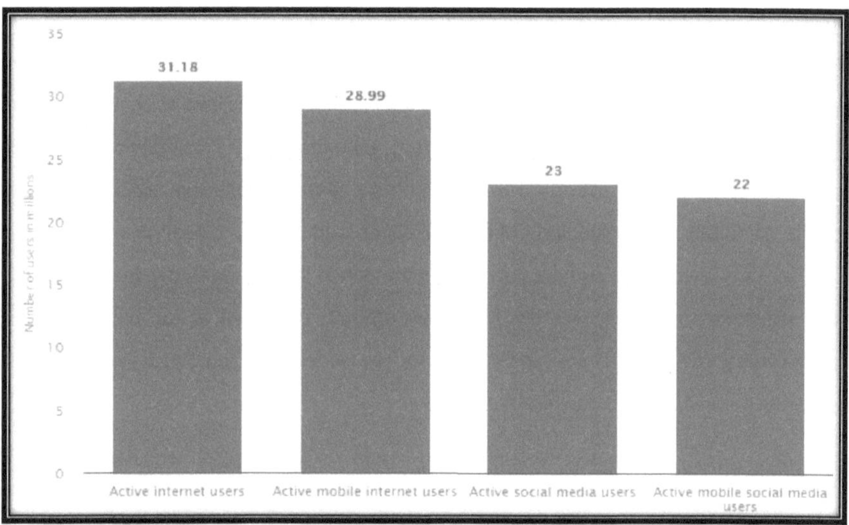

Figure 2: Internet users within South Africa (Statista, 2019b).

IoT has begun to play a crucial role in the introduction of smart cities, such as traffic monitoring, wastewater management, smart agriculture, such as food safety monitoring and smart farming (Cao et al., 2016). The Smart City Playbook, a report documenting the best practices of cities around the world, has named Cape Town the smartest city in Africa (Lourie, 2017). The envisioned economic opportunities that can be experienced through IoT have subsequently given rise to increased investment in smart devices and autonomous services (Conti et al., 2018). The International Data Corporation (IDC) estimates that 33% of South African organisations will be placing significant investment in IoT by 2020 (Mzekandaba, 2016). Another study discovered that other developing countries in Asia have experienced increased growth in the adoption of IoT objects and this increase is expected to grow by an average of 16% over the next five years (Matt, Becker, Kolbeck, & Hess, 2019), emphasising the importance of such technology within developing countries. However, "security issues such as privacy, access control, secure communication and secure storage of data are becoming significant challenges in IoT environments" (Conti et al., 2018; p.544).

2.8.   Future Directions

By 2017 the number of IoT devices connected through machine-to-machine (M2M) were estimated at around 8.4 billion worldwide (Li, Da Xu & Zhao, 2018), by 2020 this number will increase to 50 billion (Irshad, 2016). Many individuals will realise that IoT can improve and enhance their daily living experiences, but concerns will still remain about privacy issues of IoT (Lee, Bae & Kim, 2017). IoT devices were previously used as bots rather than more conventional hosts to generate massive amounts of attack traffic, making platforms such as Twitter, Netflix and Reddit unusable across Europe and the United States (Jerkins, 2017). Bertino and Islam (2017) explain that the attacks were not a surprise because of the heterogeneous nature of IoT devices, while going on to state that IoT systems will continue to be susceptible to attacks because many devices do not have well-defined perimeters, which continuously change due to the mobility aspects of the devices. Current market forces and regulatory requirements required to manage and mitigate such insecurities do not exist, leaving individuals susceptible to attacks (Jerkins, 2017).

A reality where IoT is considered a key driver, contains many challenges, especially from a security and privacy perspective because pre-existing security primitives cannot act as a holistic solution, due to the different standards and various communication stacks involved (Iqbal, Olaleye, & Bayoumi, 2017). Individuals must accept that they need to be ready to alter their privacy expectations, to account for the unpredictable realities brought forward by IoT, as it will become increasingly more difficult to define, enforce and sustain universally accepted legal privacy standards (Thierer, 2013).

The following sections depict how the hypotheses within this study were formulated, in which previous studies were used as the underpinnings for the development of a structured model. As mentioned, the privacy calculus posits that privacy issues are exacerbated by the continuous trade-off between improved service delivery (benefits) and the subsequent sacrifice of one's privacy (cost/risk), which is a consequence of the 'information age' (Norberg, Horne, & Horne, 2007). However, research depicts that the decision to disclose personal information is multifaceted (Williams, 2018). The privacy calculus assumes that people act in a rational manner, whereas behavioural economics accentuates that a decision-making process can be influenced by other factors (Beuker, 2016; Williams, 2018). Besides the benefit-risk trade-off postulated by the privacy calculus, the continuous sacrifice of information is significantly influenced by an individual's level of privacy knowledge/awareness (Macada & Luciano, 2010; Williams, 2018). Generally, individuals are more likely to be pro data sharing if they are consciously involved in the data exchange process (Barth et al., 2019), although those that are ill-informed about data handling and lack a sufficient level of privacy knowledge are more prone to information disclosure (Barth et al., 2019).

Another factor relates to information sensitivity, in which the type of information being collected can determine an individual's willingness to disclose (Marwick & Hargittai, 2018). Social/peer influence has been associated with information disclosure over SNS such as Facebook (Beuker, 2016). The perceived benefit in using IoT is subjective (Krasnova et al., 2010); especially due to the autonomous manner in which IoT objects are being deployed, where a device can "sense" and record personal information (such as health data), which represents an entirely new threat to individuals' privacy (Conti et al., 2018). Lopez et al. (2017) support this claim by going on to emphasise that IoT objects are being deployed to collect individual's personal information without them even noticing, where many are unaware that the process is even occurring (Taddicken, 2014). Due to the nature of IoT, situations may arise where individuals become suspicious of prospective benefits, which intensifies privacy concern as well as perceived risk (PwC Health Research Institute, 2014). Subsequently initiating self-withdrawal tendencies and a reluctance to divulge information (Shibchurn & Van, 2014).

When an individual discloses personal information about himself/herself it is often referred to as self-disclosure (Beuker, 2016). Self-disclosure can be defined as the communication of personal/private information (Bauer, Schmid & Strauss, 2018). "In addition to the amount of information, the diversity and quality of personal information shared is becoming increasingly important, so the users' perceived risk worsens. Hence, information sensitivity and trust play a critical role in determining information disclosure behaviour" (Kim et al., 2019, p. 274). Information sensitivity is the belief that if particular information were made public knowledge, then it would be regarded as a loss of privacy (Kim et al., 2019). It has been established in prior research that the type of data being requested of an individual, can subsequently influence disclosure (von Entreß-Fürsteneck, Buchwald, & Urbach, 2019). Doig (2016) agrees, stating that individuals are willing to provide information when the sensitivity and importance of that information is valued at a low sensitivity; such as gender, age and marital status, while going on to explain that the greater sensitivity the information holds, such as financial records and passwords, the less likely disclosure will occur. Conversely, the privacy paradox implies that individuals do not always carry out rational decisions with regards to their information disclosure (Keith et al., 2013).

Hypothesis 1: Information sensitivity influences willingness to disclose personal information.

A general consensus within literature orientated around privacy, is that perceived benefits, perceived risks and privacy concerns are key influencers in privacy behaviours and intentions to self-disclosure (Libaque-Saenz et al., 2016). Individuals are concerned about the inappropriate collection, storage, profiling and use of their personal information for unintended purposes without their consent, as well as who has access to it, who controls it and what it is used for (Aleisa & Renaud, 2017a; Keith et al., 2013; Ortiz et al., 2018). Libaque-Saenz et al. (2016) agree, stating that individuals harbour scepticism towards service providers because of the possibility that their personal information could potentially be used without authorisation, therefore, leading to heightened privacy concerns towards potential risk. The news that iPhones and Android devices 'secretly' track user information and that a large majority; nearly half of iPhone applications can do so, further amplifies the growing concern of an impending 'surveillance society' (Novotny et al., 2015; Sutanto, Palme, Tan & Phang, 2013). The data collected by IoT devices in such instances where benefits seemingly outweigh potential risk often consists of sensitive information that third parties might be interested in (Henze et al., 2016).

There have been instances in which wearable fitness devices have already provided information on the pregnancy status of their female owners (Brinson & Rutherford, 2016; Williams, Nurse & Creese, 2016), while smart TVs have been susceptible to eavesdropping on conversations (Niemietz, Somorovsky, Mainka & Schwenk, 2015). Xu et al. (2011) mentions another instance of increased privacy concern, in which individuals were concerned about their information being collected and used to perform personalisation. However, research posits that the frequent use of an internet-based platform or device, results in individuals expressing lower concern of privacy and security and they are subsequently more likely to share their information on that specific network (Kisekka et al., 2013). Kowatsch and Maass (2012) incorporated the Utility Maximisation Theory and the Privacy Calculus Model in their study, the authors argued that if IoT services and devices are perceived as useful and the higher the interest in using them exists, the lower privacy concerns will be expressed and subsequently the higher adoption rates will be.

Despite the appeal of IoT, there is a concern pertaining to potential threats to individuals' privacy in the use of devices and applications (Hallam & Zanella, 2016; Williams et al., 2017). Paradoxically the growing concern has not inhibited people from treating their privacy as a commodity (Buchwald et al., 2017) and continuously enriching IoT objects despite their concern (Conti et al., 2018), knowingly or unknowingly (Lopez et al., 2017; von Entreß-Fürsteneck, Buchwald, & Urbach, 2019). Platforms that provide individuals with multiple methods to control their information can reduce privacy concerns related to data invasion (Wang et al., 2016), however many individuals lack the skills and knowledge to manage their privacy effectively (Wu et al., 2018).

Hypothesis 2: Privacy concerns influences individuals' willingness to disclose personal information.

Section 2.9.3 and 2.9.4 focuses on the importance of perceived risks and perceived benefits (Krasnova et al., 2010; Lee, Park & Kim, 2013; Ng, 2014; Wang et al., 2016). "Perceived risk is an individual's perception of uncertainty and the adverse consequences of pursuing an activity or behaviour" (Chang, Liu & Shen, 2017, p.209). In the use of wearables, Dincelli and Zhou (2017), define privacy risk as the uncertainty individuals hold over the potential misuse or loss of control over their personal information, where these uncertainties can negatively affect those individuals' intention disclose their information. Perceived risk may affect technology adoption and usage behaviours, as the risks involved in a particular decision could impact financial, social, psychological and privacy aspects of an individual (Chang et al., 2017). Although a lack of awareness and knowledge of those risks among social media users has been documented, revealing that almost half of the respondents did not consider any risk to their privacy when sharing information online (Cheung et al., 2015). Castro and Bettencourt (2017) agree, stating that individuals who have social media profiles, are more likely to take on greater risks than those who do not. Research suggests that general privacy concerns may or may not affect users' intentions to disclose personal information (Dinev & Hart, 2006). However, privacy risk perceptions in relation to technology are considered a significant determinant in reduced intention to disclose (Keith et al., 2013).

The top risks associated to using IoT devices are; **authentication issues, identity theft, eavesdropping** through man in the middle attacks (MITM) and **malicious code injection** (Alladi, Chamola, Sikdar & Choo, 2020; Shepherd, Petitcolas, Akram & Markantonakis, 2017; Williams, McMahon, Samtani, Patton & Chen, 2017). IoT can invade users' privacy on an unprecedented level, which could be vulnerable to potential technical and user exploits (Wiiliams et al., 2017). As mentioned, one of the tops risks of IoT relates to authentication issues through vulnerabilities such as, unauthorised device pairing, permitting weak passwords and the absence of multi-factor authentication (Shepherd et al., 2017). Compromised authentication can lead to unauthorised use of banking facilities and other personal applications, as well as pairing with sensitive devices associated to healthcare (Shepherd et al., 2017). Another documented risk relates to eavesdropping through devices that lack sufficient encryption capabilities between the device and the backend server (Alladi et al., 2020). Alladi et al. (2020) goes on to mention growing concerns around malicious code injection attacks on IoT devices, which popularly happened to Google's Nest Thermostat, where the intention was to create a botnet out of the thermostat to control an entire home network, which could result in profiling of individuals through illegal surveillance within a compromised house.

Research stipulates that without the necessary of knowledge and understanding of these risks, individuals will leave themselves open to privacy invasion (Crossler & Bélanger, 2017). Based on the risks mentioned and the potential consequences which could occur if any were to be inflicted on an individual, this study follows the same facets to perceived risks as Buchwald et al. (2017) and Kisekka et al. (2013). The authors assume that privacy risks are a negative influence on willingness to disclose information, specifically in the context of IoT, where individuals share personal activity and body data (Buchwald et al., 2017; Kisekka et al., 2013).

Hypothesis 3: A higher level of perceived privacy risk lowers the willingness to provide personal information.

2.9.4. Perceived Benefits

Both extrinsic and intrinsic factors influence behavioural intentions (Yang, Yu, Zo, & Choi, 2016). "Extrinsic benefits are functional and utilitarian, while intrinsic benefit perceptions result from fun and playfulness for their own sake" (Yang, et al., 2016, p. 257). Within privacy and security research individuals are extrinsically motivated to adopt preventative behaviour that is aimed at securing their privacy, resulting in the benefit of avoiding information compromise (Yoo, Hand & Huang, 2012). Individuals feel that doing something to achieve utilitarian outcomes is equally as fulfilling as doing something which may reap certain rewards/tangible benefits (Yoo, Hand & Huang, 2012).

This study focuses on intrinsic benefits, in which the creation of niche products and personalised services, as well as saving time in performing activities are a few benefits that can arise through individuals sharing their personal information (Carignani & Gemmo, 2018). IoT devices, specifically wearable can enable benefits including fitness-data inspired lifestyle, as wells a virtual and augmented reality (Lee, Lee, Egelman & Wagner, 2016). Perceived benefits such as the abovementioned, are expected to positively influence behavioural intentions to disclose personal information (Libaque-Saenz et al., 2016). The perceived benefits discussed in this section relate to personalised services, self-presentation and enjoyment (Beldad & Hegner, 2017; Krasnova et al., 2010; Ng, 2014).

2.9.4.1.   *Personalised Services*

Personalised services are considered the most tangible benefit in relation to self-disclosure, where personalised services act as an incentive for individuals to divulge their personal information to organisations (Chellappa, Sin & Jia, 2014). This notion is posited by Xu et al. (2011), stating that Individuals have been documented to provide significant amounts of personal information in pursuit of personalised services or information access. This trend of information disclosure has continued due to the rising demand of personalised services in various sectors, including healthcare, education, sport and entertainment (Beldad & Hegner, 2017; Buchwald et al., 2017). Personalised services have been associated with a variety of financial benefits as well, such as discounts, rebates and vouchers (Buchwald et al., 2017).

Personalised services involve the collection and use of individuals' personal information to tailor services and contents for each specific individual (Wang et al., 2016). Individuals show a sufficient level of willingness to provide their personal details with the expectation of receiving improved personalised services in return (Wang et al., 2016). IoT devices can collect a lot of data about individuals, which can both directly and indirectly reveal their activities, habits and location (Blythe & Johnson, 2018). Through the use of analytics, organisations profit from the information collected, through targeted advertising or selling the information to third party organisations (Blythe & Johnson, 2018).

2.9.4.2.   *Self-Presentation*

Self-presentation refers to establishing the desired image of oneself (Kokolakis, 2017). Perceived benefits are enablers of information disclosure (Kisekka et al., 2013), a few of these benefits have been identified as maintaining relationships, enjoyment and self-presentation (Kisekka et al., 2013). Self-presentation is viewed as an indirect form of communication behaviour in which individuals are subsequently motivated to disclose personal information, with the aim of constructing and maintaining a desired public image (Lee-Won, Shim, Joo, & Park, 2014; Rui & Stefanone, 2013). The incorporation of IoT devices such as smartwatches can be viewed as a means of establishing a desired image of oneself within society, as a smartwatch can be considered a symbol of fashion and wealth (Choi & Kim, 2016).

2.9.4.3.   *Enjoyment*

Anticipation of benefits, such as enjoyment and social acceptance can motivate individuals to reveal private information (Dincelli & Zhou, 2017; Krasnova, Veltri & Günther, 2012; Yang et al., 2016). Krasnova et al. (2012) goes on to state that while potential benefits such as, improved connectedness and self-enhancement have been identified as outcomes that individuals may receive through self-disclosure over social media, the role of enjoyment is the most significant as individuals seek entertainment over online interactions. The statement has been further supported by Chen and Sharma (2015) and Liu, Min, Zhai, and Smyth (2016), going on to state that enjoyment is a more power predictor of participation and disclosure, than perceived usefulness. Cheung et al. (2015) state that if something stimulates enjoyment for individuals then there is a greater likelihood that those individuals will reveal personal information. The authors go on to highlight that individuals are continually becoming more reliant on technology, leading them to enjoy the convenience that those technologies (i.e. smartphones) bring, while simultaneously paying little to no attention to the associated risks involved (Cheung et al., 2015). In which service providers elicit or convince users that they need to disclose particular information to achieve further enjoyment (Beuker, 2016).

Hypothesis 4: A higher level of perceived benefit increases the willingness to provide personal information.

2.9.5. Social Influence

Social influence refers to the influence that social groups may have on an individual's attitudes, beliefs and behaviours (Hein, Jodoin, Rauschnabel & Ivens, 2018; Wang, Meister, & Gray, 2013). Previous research (Cheung et al., 2015; Das, Kramer, Dabbish, & Hong, 2014; Li, 2011; Zhou, 2011), established that social influence is a critical factor that determines individuals' behaviour, specifically in the context of social networking. People rely on their friends and families for guidance when it comes to decisions regarding digital privacy and security (Aljallad et al., 2019). Social influence consists of three processes: **compliance, identification** and **internalisation** (Zhou & Li, 2014). **Compliance** refers to an individual complying with the opinions of others, in an attempt to gain a reward or avoid a negative outcome (Zhou & Li, 2014). **Identification** refers to the way in which an individual views himself/herself, with respect to a group's defining features (Zhou & Li, 2014). **Internalisation** represents how an individual incorporates the opinions of others into their own beliefs (Zhou & Li, 2014). However, social risks may arise through the use of self-disclosure technology, Dincelli and Zhou (2017) state that the desire is dependent on the response of others and that sharing physical activities on various platforms may led to negative comparisons (Dincelli & Zhou, 2017). Social influence can affect technology usage, for instance the use of smart glasses can evoke a negative effect because of their ability to record other people without their knowledge and subsequently infringe on their privacy (Hei n et al., 2018).

"Social influence is a major avenue for adopting online behaviours in general and privacy practices in particular" (Mendel & Toch, 2017, p.1), because individuals want to establish or maintain relationships with others (Li, 2011). With respect to IoT, users can share data with service providers, which enable the users to connect to their social group e.g. family and friends, on social media or dedicated platforms such as Nike+, which can significantly influence usage and disclosure (von Entreß-Fürsteneck, Buchwald, & Urbach, 2019). An individual's privacy behaviour can be affected by others' willingness, this is referred to as the 'herding effect' (Wu, et al., 2018). Herding relates to behavioural patterns of an individual correlating with those around them, where an individual would more likely disclose personal information if those in their close social groupings do (Wu, et al., 2018). Individuals desire others' approval and may use self-disclosure as a strategy to achieve approval within their social groupings (Dincelli & Zhou, 2017).

Aljallad et al. (2019) stress the innate impulse for individuals to seek advice or model behaviours from friends and/or family when new situations or uncertainties arise. Social influence/peer pressure should be investigated because of the number of IoT devices and applications that are used alongside social networks, as opposed to rational decision of the privacy calculus; being a benefit-risk analysis (Beuker, 2016; Das, Kramer, Dabbish, & Hong, 2014). Individuals act within social environments and therefore social pressures can be assumed to be have an influence on information disclosure (Beuker, 2016). Williams, Nurse & Creese (2016) put forward the importance that social influence plays in this regard, citing the example where individuals in the 1980s stored personal data in their homes, whereas individuals now share their lives on social media and cloud-based platforms.

Hypothesis 5: A higher level of Social influence positively influences willingness to disclose personal information.

2.9.6. Privacy Knowledge

Literature has illustrated that individuals may not actually realise or know when they are giving their information away when using smart devices (Belanger & Crossler, 2019), where significant amounts of data are being collected by third parties through the applications running in the background (Aljallad et al., 2019). An important component of this research is that individuals have various understandings, differences of opinion and knowledge about privacy and security, where "these differences subsequently create a knowledge gap that influences individuals' disclosure behaviours, putting their information at risk" (Crossler & Bélanger, 2017; p. 4071). Research documents that many individuals that use IoT devices and services are unaware of the various threats that could affect them, such as the Mirai Botnet, which targets and compromises many IoT devices within a particular area to generate massive amounts of traffic used to disrupt networks and platforms (Fremantle, Aziz & Kirkham, 2017; Jerkins, 2017; Wei, 2016).

The problem with the privacy paradox is that most individuals lack the necessary cognitive ability to calculate the trade-off correctly, while many are inhibited by a lack of sufficient information in this regard (Kokolakis, 2017). From an emotive stance, Boehmer, LaRose, Rifon, Alhabash and Cotten (2015) state that by simply mentioning negative consequences, referring to fear appeals in relation to privacy and security concerns, as having a limited impact on human behaviour. While the method itself has been documented to inhibit safe behaviour rather than ensure it, in which people may suppress their fear rather than placing importance on becoming privacy averse (Boehmer et al., 2015; Lawson, Yeo, Yu & Greene, 2016). Crossler and Bélanger (2017) explain that in the context of information security and privacy, the combination of perceived ability and actual knowledge to understand current threats, are both needed to effectively experience sufficient protection. Therefore, privacy decisions made are constrained by incomplete information, lack of knowledge and bounded rationality (Kokolakis, 2017).

Individuals that believe their information privacy and security knowledge to be above average have a higher level of conviction to safeguard their personal information (Stajkovic & Luthans, 1998). That being said, the overconfidence associated with that conviction has been documented to be counterintuitive, resulting in individuals gaining more exposure to the internet and becoming less concerned with the risks associated to their personal information through their online interactions (Chen & Chen, 2015), subsequently leading to a lack of preventative behaviour (Crossler & Belanger). William et al. (2017) state that IoT devices are continuously collecting data, these constrained devices communicate with other appliances, while their owners have little understanding of how this occurs. Individuals tend to reveal more information than they might desire because of their incomplete understanding of permissions management and associated consequences of granting access to their data, through various applications, devices and platforms (Pu & Grossklags, 2016). The problem lies in the fact that companies are collecting the data and sharing or selling them to third parties (Vitak, Liao, Kumar, Zimmer & Kritikos, 2018). Vitak et al. (2018) goes on to state that although the data may seem innocuous, like that of fitness information, the continuous flow of data coupled with other data can reveal detailed insights about and individual's health and habits.

From a bounded rationality perspective, incomplete information and information asymmetry suggests that decision-making is constrained by a lack of knowledge (Hallam & Zanella, 2016). The lack of awareness and knowledge of individuals will subsequently distort concern around privacy and hinder decision-making related to personal disclosure (Vitak et al., 2018; Wu, Zhang, Cui & Wang, 2018).

Hypothesis 6: Privacy Knowledge influences Privacy Concern.
Hypothesis 7: Individuals with a higher level of privacy knowledge are less likely to disclose personal information than those with a low level of privacy knowledge.

2.9.7. Self-withdrawal

"Individuals strive to attain their ideal level of privacy by applying context-specific strategies of self-disclosure and withdrawal" (Trepte et al., 2017, p.2). In an attempt to extend the privacy calculus theory, Dienlin and Metzger (2016) found that previous research has not addressed the concept of self-withdrawal in a sufficient manner, where unlike self-disclosure; self-withdrawal refers adopting practices to retain information. Although it has been documented that individuals are willing to disclose information to incur potential financial rewards, at the same time, this type of benefit make some individuals suspicious that their information will be further traded with third parties (Shibchurn & Van, 2014). Hence, increasing concerns around privacy and subsequently prompting self-withdrawal tendencies and a reluctance to divulge information (Shibchurn & Van, 2014). Crossler and Belanger (2017) state that if personal information can be fraudulently accessed (such as financial information), then individuals are more than likely to refrain from disclosing their information. When privacy risks are considered too high to be offset by perceived benefits, individuals become prone to limiting their self-disclosure tendencies or engage in self-withdrawing behaviour (Ranzini, Etter, Lutz & Vermeulen, 2017). Therefore, individuals establish privacy rules for both information disclosure and information withholding when several situations arise (Dienlin & Metzger, 2016).

Hypothesis 8: The more concerned people are regarding their privacy, the more they will engage in acts of self-withdrawal.

Hypothesis 9: A higher level of perceived privacy risk, the more likely people will engage in acts of self-withdrawal.

2.10. Summary of Hypotheses

The hypotheses mentioned within this study will be tested to either confirm or reject the claims. The table below represents the hypotheses for this research, they will be tested and expressed through statistical analysis from data captured through the research instrument. The hypotheses form the basis of the research model displayed above and will be tested to meet the aim of this study; to understand the cause of personal disclosure in the use of IoT. Below is a list of each hypothesis as well as its related null hypothesis, used to reject or support the hypotheses.

#	Hypotheses
H_1	Information sensitivity influences willingness to disclose personal information.
H_2	Privacy concern influences individuals' willingness to disclose personal information.

H₃	Perceived privacy risk negatively influences the willingness to provide personal information.
H₄	The more people expect benefits by using IoT, the higher their willingness to provide personal information.
H₅	Social influence positively influences willingness to disclose personal information.
H₆	Privacy Knowledge influences Privacy Concern.
H₇	Privacy knowledge influences information disclosure.
H₈	The more concerned people are regarding their privacy, the more they will engage in acts of self-withdrawal.
H₉	The more people expect risk in the use of IoT, the more likely people will engage in acts of self-withdrawal.

Table 1: List of Hypotheses.

2.11. Conceptual Model

The systematic literature conducted did not reveal any existing theoretical model that comprehensively matched the variables used within this study, so a conceptual model was drawn up based upon key themes extracted from previous literature and adapted to fit this study. Several studies have focused on intentions to disclose personal information in the use of SNS or mobile phones (Beuker, 2016; Hallam & Zanella, 2017; Krasnova et al. 2010; Wang et al.,2016; Williams, 2018). However, due to the ubiquitous nature of IoT and the manner in which data is being collected (Aljallad et al., 2019; Kim et al., 2019; Naeini et al., 2017; Williams. 2018), a combination of different variables found within multiple models were found to be better suited. The manner in which IoT continuously collects data and particularly the type of data that is collected, meant that information sensitivity had to be taken into account because as research suggests the sensitivity of the data may influence the degree of disclosure (Doig, 2016). Kim et al. (2019), Krasnova, Veltri and Günther, O. (2012) and Wang et al. (2016) based their studies off the privacy calculus, which focused on perceived benefit and perceived risk (see figure 3). Because the privacy calculus was established as the theoretical underpinning of this study, the research included both variables in the conceptual model (see figure 5).

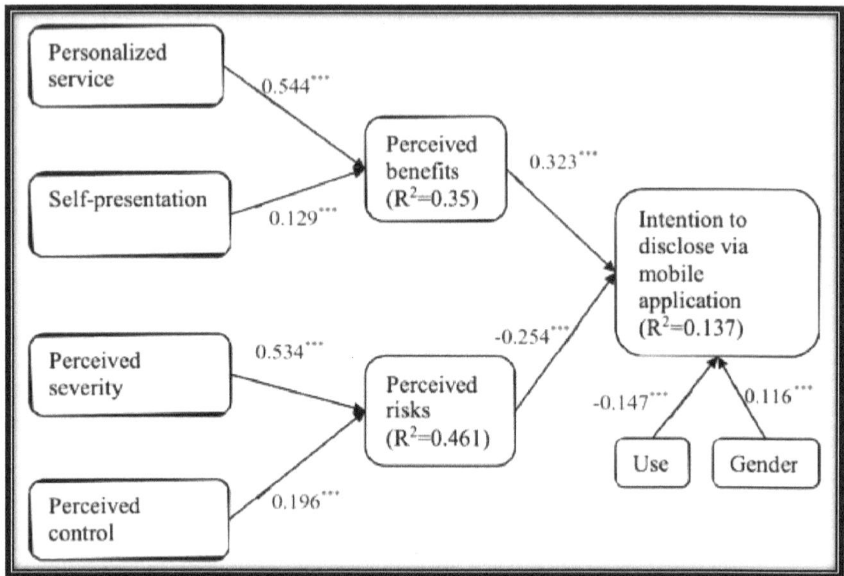

Figure 3: Research Model of Intentions to disclose via mobile application (Wang et al., 2016, p.538).

Beuker (2016) incorporated peer pressure into their study, as the author mainly focused on young adults and therefore identified peer pressure as a pivotal factor within SNS studies (see figure 4). This study included this variable but reclassified it as social influence because research illustrated that individuals' attitudes, beliefs and behaviours are influenced by their friends and/or family rather than being pressured to make a decision (Aljallad et al., 2019; Hein, Jodoin, Rauschnabel & Ivens, 2018; Wang, Meister, & Gray, 2013). Privacy concern has continuously been identified as a key factor within research pertaining to the privacy paradox and therefore, could not be overlooked (Kim & Kim, 2018). However, self-withdrawal is a fairly new topic within this focus area and thus, the models reviewed had not included it as a potential outcome within information disclosure (Dienlin & Metzger, 2016).

Another variable that many models did not include was privacy knowledge. Research indicates that that without proper knowledge or understanding of potential risk, means that an inaccurate calculation of a trade-off may occur (Kokolakis, 2017). While having limited knowledge of information security and privacy may result lack of effective protection measures (Hallam & Zanella, 2016).

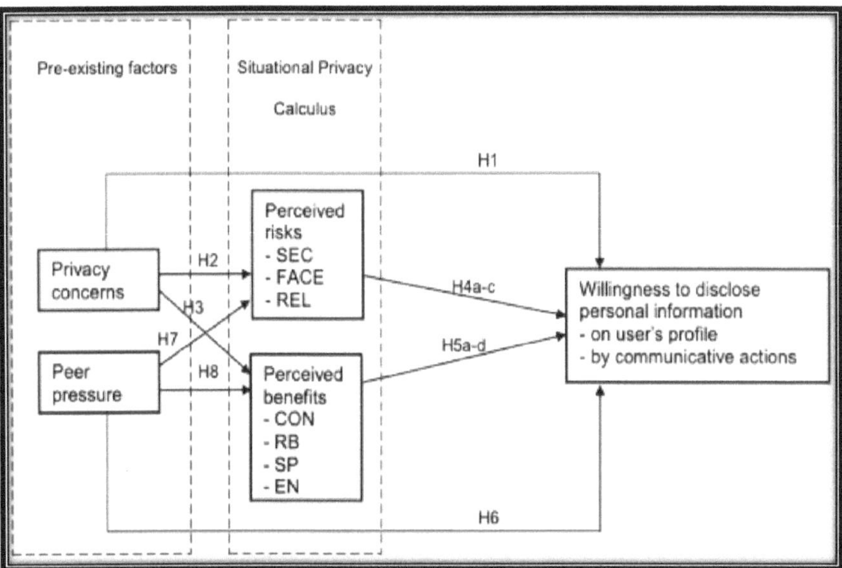

Figure 4: Research Model of Factors Influencing Disclosure of Personal Information Among German and Dutch SNS Users (Beuker, 2016, p.20).

Figure 5 below, depicts the conceptual model developed within this study. The hypotheses mentioned earlier in section 2 of this study are illustrated in the conceptual model. The model explains potential factors that influence information disclosure. As mentioned previously, the conceptual model was developed through the combination of multiple variables highlighted in several previous studies, which researched self-disclosure in various contexts (Beuker, 2016; Cheung et al., 2015; Crossler & Bélanger, 2014; Dienlin & Metzger, 2016; Hajli & Lin, 2016; Kehr, Wentzel, Kowatsch & Fleisch, 2015; Kokolakis, 2017; Krasnova et al., 2010; Libaque-Saenz et al., 2016; Wang et al., 2016). The variables within the conceptual model, in combination with the privacy calculus will assist in answering the research questions and achieving the research objectives.

The independent variables in relation to the dominant dependent variable are privacy concern, social influence, information sensitivity, privacy knowledge and characteristics of the privacy calculus which are split into perceived benefits and perceived risks. Intentions to disclose personal information in the use of IoT has been set as the dominant dependent variable. Aside from the main purpose of the study, there were two other dependent variables associated to the conceptual model; privacy concern was listed as a dependent variable to measure the relationship between it and privacy knowledge, while self-withdrawal was listed as a dependent variable to measure the counteraction of intentions to disclose personal information in the use of IoT.

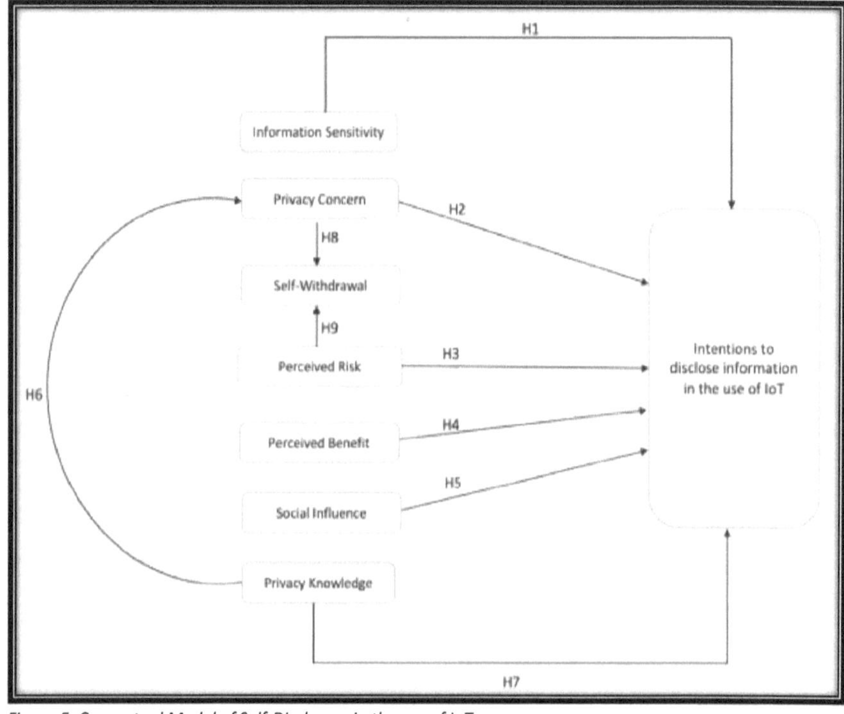

Figure 5: Conceptual Model of Self-Disclosure in the use of IoT.

2.12. Conclusion of Literature Review

The IoT refers to everyday physical objects being able to connect to the Internet, identify themselves with other devices and engage in seamless and automated data exchange (Kietzmann, Pitt, McCarthy & Schau, 2018). Prior research has shown over-disclosure of personal information to common practice amongst Internet users (Preibusch, Krol, & Beresford, 2013). With the new methods of data collection that the IoT brings, new privacy challenges are being created (Naeini et al., 2017). Although there are various factors that influence disclosure (Krasnova et al., 2010), even individuals with sufficient information and understanding of associated risks, are likely to trade long-term privacy for short-term benefits (Wu et al., 2018). Below is a summary of the perceived risks and perceived benefits mentioned in sections 2.9.3 and 2.9.4 respectively:

Perceived Risks	Perceived Benefits
Authentication Issues	Personalised Services
Identity Theft	Self-presentation
Eavesdropping	Enjoyment
Malicious Code Injection	

Table 2: Summary of Perceived Risks and Perceived Benefits.

Previous research relating to personal information disclosure primarily focuses on disclosing information on SNSs, e-commerce platforms and mobile phones (Buchwald et al., 2017; Keith et al., 2013), with IoT related research being in its infancy (Williams et al., 2017). Dominant aspects in information disclosure studies has been orientated around perceived benefits and perceived risks (i.e. the privacy calculus), relatively less attention has been given towards social influence or self-withdrawal and the value individuals attribute to different types of information (Cheung et al., 2015; Dienlin & Metzger, 2016). The literature reviewed predominantly investigated the privacy paradox within Northern America, therefore, the conclusions made surrounding the paradox may differ in the context of SA, due to culture and socio-economic aspects within SA (Williams, 2018). Another insight revealed through the literature reviewed is that student samples were often solicited in research relating to the privacy paradox (Sharma & Crossler, 2014; Wang et al., 2016), with little consideration of the general public and real-life scenarios (Williams et al., 2017).

The high-risk associated with IoT devices presents researchers with various avenues in which to study information disclosure decisions due to the unique and emerging nature of potential risks (Keith, Thompson, Hale, Lowry & Greer, 2013). From a privacy perspective most studies have been focused on developing an understanding of what privacy actually means in the context of IoT, or what mechanisms can be put in place to protect data such as data encryption (Román-Castro, López, & Gritzalis, 2018). Although, there are a lack of studies orientated around the privacy paradox in relation to IoT (Williams, 2018). As the field of privacy expands, future research should take into account privacy behaviour, perceptions and the privacy paradox (Williams et al., 2017). Therefore, there is a growing importance to gain a better understanding of how the public make sense of privacy risks in relation to storing and sharing of their data (Castro & Bettencourt, 2017), as well as the privacy paradox within the context of IoT (Williams et al., 2017). By identifying key factors that influence individuals' willingness to disclose personal information in the use of IoT, conclusions can be made around privacy related opinions and actions within the South African landscape (Williams, et al., 2017).

There is a need to provide explanations of public opinions surrounding the paradox because this state of affairs distorts public actions, their will and overall opinion towards privacy (Baek, 2014). Without practical analysis of the privacy paradox, IoT might increase potential privacy risk (Williams et al., 2017). Such research might grow in importance within SA, where investment in IoT continues to grow, both from a consumer and business perspective (Mzekandaba, 2016; Statista, 2019a). SA experiences the third highest number of internet-based crimes in the world, putting individuals' privacy at risk but privacy related issues have not attracted the attention it deserves (Kritzinger, 2017). Therefore, this research is well-placed, considering current and future investment into IoT and the potential risk to individuals' privacy due to the high-level of cyber-crime within the country. This research aims to contribute to the information privacy body of knowledge, particularly in the fields related to IoT and the privacy paradox. By shedding light on the potential paradox within SA and the reason(s) behind the paradox, individuals can potentially understand why they disclose their personal information over IoT and if it's worth it.

3. Research Design and Methodology

3.1. Introduction

"Research design is a comprehensive plan for data collection in an empirical research project" (Bhattacherjee, 2012, p.35). According to research practices, the research design aims at providing a holistic overview of the research process, including the plans, guidelines, procedures and roadmap to be undertaken by the researcher(s) (Myers, 2009). This section follows the research process outline by Saunders et al. (2009), comprising of the following sections: section 3.2. discusses the research philosophy adopted; section 3.3. is orientated around the research methodology, which includes the research strategy, the purpose of the research, the research approach, the target population and sampling frame as well as the research instrument and analysis techniques; section 3.4. discusses the limitations of this study; section 3.5. discusses ethics and confidentially issues associated with this study; and section 3.6. illustrates the research timeframe.

3.2. Research Philosophy

Research philosophies play a significant role within the research process, influencing the research strategy and the methods a researcher chooses as part of that strategy, because the adopted research philosophy contains various assumptions on the way in which researchers view the world (Saunders, et al., 2009). There are two assumptions that exist regarding philosophical standpoints; ontological stance and epistemological stance (Ajumobi, 2014), which is discussed in section 3.2.1. and section 3.2.2.

3.2.1. Ontology

"Ontology is concerned with nature of reality" (Saunders et al., 2009, p. 110). In research there are two dominant ontological stances: objectivism and subjectivism (Saunders et al., 2009). Orlikowski and Baroudi (1991) state that these two stances essentially propose two schools of thought with regards to the way in which the world is viewed; where the world is independent or dependent of humans. This study adopted an objectivistic stance, where this ontological stance assumes that social entities (researchers) exist in a reality external to social actors, where the social actors (humans) can be characterised and measured (Bryman & Bell, 2011; Saunders, et al., 2009).

An Epistemological stance relates to the way in which a researcher perceives the sources, processes and interpretations of knowledge (Crotty, 1998; Koskinen, Pihlanto & Vanharanta, 2003), essentially epistemology is concerned with how the researcher collates knowledge (Killam, 2013). Within social science research there exists three dominant epistemological stances: interpretivist, critical realist stances and positivistic (Saunders et al., 2009). The critical realist stance insinuates that although people could be constrained by several cultural, political and social factors, they should be able to change their socio-economic situations (Bhattacherjee, 2012). Therefore, researchers that adopt this stance are often associated with the emancipation of others and human empowerment issues (Cavana, Delahaye & Sekeran, 2001). The second epistemological stance is referred to as Interpretivism, which follows the assumption that social reality is determined through critically analysing and concisely understand the meaning and purpose humans associate to their actions through interpretive methods, such as shared meanings, language, artefacts and consciousness (Bhattacherjee, 2012; Klein & Myers, 1999; Saunders et al., 2009). Saunders et al. (2009) elaborate on the matter by stipulating that interpretivism is not a stance that assumes understandings can be objectively measured, unlike positivism; rather interpretivism is established on the assumption that the most effective way of gathering substantial knowledge on the meanings people assign to a particular phenomenon is through subjectively immersing oneself into that reality. Therefore, interpretivist research relates to a researcher interacting with respondents to gain understandings and to conceptualise respondents' goals (Walsham, 1995).

The final epistemological stance is positivism (Bhattacherjee, 2012). The positivistic stance postulates that knowledge is readily available and can be observed and measured objectively (Dikow, Hasan, Kosch, Brunie & Sornin, 2015). The underlying epistemological stance of this research was positivistic as the aim of this study was to objectively understand the cause of the Privacy Paradox within the context of IoT, which subsequently looks at information disclosure relating to IoT within SA. Positivism is orientated around extrapolating information and knowledge through direct observation of entities that are considered to be observable (Green, Camilli & Elmore, 2012). Saunders et al. (2009) state that only facts and data gained through observation are considered sufficient within this epistemological paradigm. Orlikowski and Baroudi (1991) state that positivistic studies are associated with understanding relationships within research phenomena, through quantifiable measures of variables or hypotheses testing from an established sample, which are usually investigated through the use of structured instruments. This stance is in line with this study, where the hypotheses stated earlier in this document were tested, with the aim of answering the research question, in an objective manner.

3.3. Research Methodology

The research methodology encompasses the various activities that a researcher employs to derive reliable outcomes and describes the tasks conducted throughout the research process (Babbie, 2015; Mingers, 2001). The research methodology should provide an accurate explanation of the adopted methods used for collecting, measuring and analysing data incorporated within the research process (Creswell & Clark, 2007). The following section comprises of the adopted research approach, the research strategy, as well as the techniques that were used when conducting data collection.

3.3.1. Research Approach

There are two research approaches associated with scientific research: inductive research and deductive research (Bhattacherjee, 2012). Bhattacherjee (2012) and Thomas (2006) state that deductive research involves constructing hypotheses or propositions based on established theories or prior theoretical work, where these hypotheses or propositions are then extensively tested, resulting in them being either confirmed or rejected. This study adopted the deductive approach, where the goal of the research is not to infer theoretical assumptions based on the data analysed but rather to test the conceptual framework, against the data collected, to find support or contradictions against the existing theory (Ajumobi, 2014; Saunders et al., 2009; Thomas, 2006). The deductive approach has been well-documented in studies that have incorporated the survey strategy (Saunders et al., 2009). The literature review conducted within this study assisted in the development of a conceptual model, which led to the development of the hypotheses that was tested using quantitative measures, with the aim of answering the research questions and addressing the research objectives.

3.3.2. Research Strategy

The term 'qualitative' has been associated with any form of data collection technique (such as an interview) or data analysis procedure (such as categorising data) that generates or uses non-numerical data. In contrast, 'quantitative' is synonymous with data collection techniques (such as a questionnaire), or data analysis procedure (such as graphs or statistics), that generates or uses numerical data. (Saunders, Lewis, & Thornhill, 2015). Quantitative research makes use of statistical analysis where researchers either reject the hypotheses or establish the effect of the research. Each hypothesis needs to be addressed individually during the analysis phase (Soiferman, 2010). This research adopted a quantitative method to data collection. Quantitative research can consist of experiments and/or survey research (Bhattacherjee, 2012), the researcher decided to incorporate the survey method with the use of an online questionnaire.

Bhattacherjee (2012) explains that research which incorporates a survey strategy includes the use of standardised questionnaires or interviews to collect data about social entities in a systematic way, with the aim of determining various preferences, thoughts and behaviours. A survey strategy is "usually associated with the deductive approach" (Saunders et al., 2009, p. 144). Bhattacherjee (2012), Saunders et al. (2009) and Glasow (2005) go on to elaborate that the strategy is suitable for the collection of data from a sizeable population such as that of a country, in a feasible manner. A survey strategy can reduce the likelihood of coverage errors arising (Schaefer & Dillman, 1998). The survey strategy is used in quantitative research, whereby the data can be analysed using descriptive and inferential statistics, subsequently leading to the uncovering of possible reasons for relationships between particular variables (Saunders et al., 2009).

The use of a survey strategy in combination with an online questionnaire is suitable for this study, due to their inherent strengths, such as being able to measure unobservable data such as preferences, beliefs and behaviour from a population size that may be too large to observe directly (Bhattacherjee, 2012). The suitability of this strategy is furthered acknowledged by its alignment of the chosen philosophical stance, in which it enables the researcher to collect data in an objective manner, while being suitable for descriptive, exploratory, or explanatory research (Bhattacherjee, 2012; Saunders et al., 2009). However, there are weaknesses that must be acknowledged when using a survey strategy, which can affect the inferences derived within the study, such as non-response bias, social desirability bias and sampling bias (Bhattacherjee, 2012), which will be discussed in a later section.

3.3.3. *Purpose of research*

The research purpose can be categorised into three types: exploratory, descriptive and explanatory (Bhattacherjee, 2012; Saunders, et al., 2009), where the research would be orientated around trying to: explore a new phenomenon, describe a social phenomenon or explain why something occurs (Ajumobi, 2014; Neuman, 1994; Saunders et al., 2009). The purpose of this study was to proactively collect information in a methodical and robust manner to understand the drivers of the privacy paradox within SA, with the aim of gaining an enhanced understanding of why individuals disclose personal information. Therefore, this research adopted an explanatory research method. Explanatory research attempts to "connect the dots in research, by identifying causal factors and outcomes of the target phenomenon" (Bhattacherjee, 2012, p. 6). "The emphasis in explanatory research is to study a situation or a problem in order to explain the relationships between variables" (Saunders et al., 2015, p. 176).

3.4.   Population and Sampling

To make observations and statistical inferences about a population of interest for a study, a research should ensure that a statistical process of narrowing down a subset of sad population is carried out, which is referred to as a sample of the population (Bhattacherjee, 2012; Saunders et al., 2009). This section breakdowns the various aspects and steps incurred to arrive at a legitimate sample for this research.

3.4.1. *Target Population*

Saunders et al. (2009) state that if a survey strategy is adopted then the researcher(s) must specify the population and sample size. This study focused on the general public within SA, specifically looking at IoT users. The privacy paradox in relation to information disclosure decisions, should not be associated as a symptom of only young people but rather a process that concerns all ages (Kokolakis, 2017). Therefore, samples should be as representative as possible and not solely focus on convenient student respondents, but rather the research should include different groupings of people; ranging from different ages, genders, educational backgrounds, as well as both professional and non-professional individuals (Kokolakis, 2017; Williams et al., 2017). Taking this into account, this research follows Williams et al. (2017), in incorporating the general public that makes use of IoT, which provides a more representative view of those with different expertise and knowledge. This research focused on the general public within SA to be to suitable for this study, as SA embodies a huge diversity of individuals, with different economic dispensation, access to knowledge and technology and educational backgrounds (Kritzinger, 2017).

3.4.2. Sampling Frame and Sample Size

"A sample size of 30 or more will usually result in a sampling distribution for the mean that is close to a normal distribution" (Saunders et al., 2009, p. 218). Although Wang et al. (2016) had over 300 respondents, while Sharma and Crossler (2014) incorporated 252 respondents in their studies, which evaluated self-disclosure. To be as representative as possible, the current number of individuals within SA that have access to the internet served as a base population, which is estimated at 31.18 million (Statista, 2019b); from that the researcher extrapolated a meaningful sample size of 385, with a 95% confidence level through the use of the Qualtrics Sample Size Calculator (Qualtrics, 2019). Therefore, this research aimed for a sample size of above 385.

As mentioned previously, this research was conducted around the general public within SA, including students over the age of 18, as previous research considers them to form part of the general public and therefore, cannot be excluded from the study (Kokolakis, 2017). Blank, Bolsover and Dubois (2014) found that younger people are more likely to take action to protect their privacy than older individuals, although this statement holds little bearing as a study by Kokolakis (2017) documents that younger people have a tendency to disclose personal information more freely, especially on social media. Such inconsistencies should be looked at with reference to the IoT. Therefore, the sample was constricted to IoT users within SA over the age of 18. The research did not include respondents below the age of 18 as Adorjan and Ricciardelli (2019) cited that those regarded as teenagers are considered to not implement effective privacy management strategies.

3.4.3. Sampling Technique

"Sampling is the statistical process of selecting a subset (called a "sample") of a population of interest for purposes of making observations and statistical inferences about that population." (Bhattacherjee, 2012, p. 65). Within research, a sampling design can be either 'Single Stage' or 'Multistage'. 'Single Stage' sampling involves sampling a population whereby the names of potential participants are known, and specific participants are subsequently chosen (Creswell, 2013). Alternatively, Multistage (or Cluster) sampling, involves the process of identifying clusters of groups to sample to determine a feasible target population (Creswell, 2013). This research made use of a multistage method because specific members within the population are not known (Saunders et al., 2009). The initial stage set out to define the target population; race, gender and nationality were not isolating factors. Since the survey was distributed to the general public, the target population were any individuals that used IoT in SA. Validation was incorporated into the survey to enforce only respondents that stipulate that they conform to the target population (which is listed below) could answer and submit the questionnaire. This population was restricted to the following respondents:

- The individual are users of IoT devices and applications.
- The individual must be living in SA.
- The Individual must be over the age of 18.

The following stage looked at defining the sampling frame. The sampling frame is an accessible subset of the target population that a sample can be drawn from (Turner, 2003). The sampling frame were students that were in the UCT Active Directory (AD). The reason for this was that the university has a broadcast function for researchers and that helped to get the questionnaire out to respondents as quickly as possible. The final step in the sampling process is choosing a sample from the sampling frame. This research adopted simple random sampling to select random participants out of the pool of initial respondents, eliminating the need to choose sampling frame based on specific characteristics (Saunders et al., 2015).

3.5. Research Instrument

An online questionnaire was used as the research instrument, the choice of instrument was guided by the adopted ontological stance and research strategy. A survey technique coupled with the use of online questionnaires allows standardisation and aggregation of findings (Saunders et al., 2009). In information systems (IS) research, the use of survey instruments for positivist research is a tried and tested method of data collection (Church& Waclawski, 2001). Creswell (2013) states that a questionnaire enables a particular environment to be surveyed by a researcher, providing a platform for objective data gathering of opinions of individuals. The online questionnaire provides a platform in which a researcher will have the least amount of influence on participants' responses, ensuring that the data collected aligns with the ontological and epistemological stances in being objective. Therefore, in line with the research approach being positivistic, the anonymous online questionnaire was disturbed remotely to a group of individuals that shared commonality (IoT users in SA). Since the questionnaire was orientated towards individuals that made use of Internet based technologies and services, the questionnaire could be distributed remotely online.

Further, the research instrument was considered cost effective and economical in terms of cost and efficient with respect to time as the questionnaire was able to reach a large audience over a short period due to it being distributed over several SNS platforms, which correlates with cross sectional time framed studies (Bhattacherjee, 2012). The questionnaire that was used in this study, consisted of closed-ended questions based on the conceptual model and subsequent hypotheses, whereby opinions and thoughts can be extrapolated from a selection of variables (Creswell, 2013). Closed-ended questions present respondents with sets of predefined answers in relation to specific questions, this can be done through the use of Nominal and Ordinal scales (Gray, 2013). Nominal scales are generally used to compare mutually exclusive attributes, such as age, gender or profession etc. (Bhattacherjee, 2012). Alternatively, Ordinal scales measure ranked-ordered data, although the relative value of the ranked attributes cannot be fundamentally assessed (Bhattacherjee, 2012). The study adopted the Likert scale as well as the above-mentioned scales, whereby the Likert scale aims to define a respondent's extent of agreement or disagreement (Bhattacherjee, 2012).

The online questionnaire was created after analysing literature associated to the hypotheses mentioned within the literature, the questionnaire was subsequently refined after sifting through several survey studies including Aleisa and Renaud, 2017b; Bueker, 2016; Cheung et al., 2015; Hajli and Lin, 2016; Hallam and Zanella, 2017; Krasonva et al., 2010; Liu et al., 2016; Mohamed and Ahmad, 2012; Wang et al., 2016; Xu et al., 2011. The completed questionnaire is presented in **Appendix D**. Most of the items within the questionnaire are measured using a five-point Likert scale with 1 representing the lower value and 5 representing the highest value. The questionnaire consists of five sections:

- Section one: covers demographical aspects such as age, gender and educational qualification, as well as general understanding of the research topic of the respondent. This was done through multiple choice questioning.

- o Section 1 contained 1 question pertaining to overall usage of IoT through a Likert scale of 1 – 5 where 1 = Not at all and 5 = All the time.
- Section two: Measures items relating to **information sensitivity**, through a Likert scale of 1 – 5 where 1 = Strongly agree and 5 = Strongly disagree or 1 = very willing and 5 = Definitely will not.
- Section three: Measures items relating to **privacy concern**, through a Likert scale of 1 – 5 where 1 = Strongly agree and 5 = Strongly disagree.
- Section four: Looks at **privacy knowledge** about privacy, with an open-ended question.
- Section five: Measures **social influence**, through a Likert scale of 1 – 5 where 1 = Strongly agree and 5 = Strongly disagree.
- Section six: Measures **self-withdrawal**, through a Likert scale of 1 – 5 where 1 = Strongly agree and 5 = Strongly disagree.
- Section seven: Measures items relating to **perceived benefits**: personalised services and self-presentation, through a Likert scale of 1 – 5 where 1 = Strongly agree and 5 = Strongly disagree.
- Section eight: Measures **perceived risks**, through a Likert scale of 1 – 5 where 1 = Strongly agree and 5 = Strongly disagree or 1 = Very Low and 5 = Very High.
- Section nine: Measured **intentions to disclose personal information in the use of IoT**, though several Likert scales of 1-5 where 1 = Strongly agree and 5 = Strongly disagree.

3.5.1. Reliability and Validity of Research Instrument

3.5.1.1. Reliability

"Reliability refers to the degree to which the results obtained by a measurement and procedure can be replicated" (Bolarinwa, 2015, p. 195). Essentially, reliability refers to the consistency of the research process and subsequently the research paper (Saunders et al., 2015). Saunders et al. (2015), elaborates by explaining that if another researcher were able to replicate a previous study's research design and achieve similar results then the previous study would be considered reliable. To ensure reliability within this study, the internal consistency reliability test was conducted, which involves measuring the different items of a construct to test for consistency through the use of Cronbach's alpha and Dillon-Goldstein's (rho_A) (Ajumobi, 2014; Alexandrou & Chen, 2014; Hair, Hult, Ringle, & Sarstedt, 2017;

Sharma & Crossler, 2014). Secondly, pilot tests were conducted, which has been determined to assist in ensuring reliability of the research instrument (Bhattacherjee, 2012; Bolarinwa, 2015).

3.5.1.2. Pilot Testing

Pilot testing assists with discovering potential problems within the research design or instrument (Bhattacherjee, 2012). To establish the reliability of a questionnaire, researchers have conducted pilot tests (Ajumobi, 2014). The subset chosen for the pilot study consisted of UCT IS students, for convenience as this subset is presumed to understand IoT, as well as research. The pilot test aimed to gauge how understandable the research questions are, to determine the feasibility of the questions and response methods while ensuring the quality of the instrument to an accessible sample (Bhattacherjee, 2012). In the event the pilot tests are successful in unearthing any errors or ambiguity within the questionnaire, one can then proceed with the data collection process, on the intended sample population (Bhattacherjee, 2012; Saunders et al., 2009).

3.5.2. Validity

Validity refers to "how accurately the measures obtained from the research was actually quantifying what it was designed to measure" (Bolarinwa, 2015, p. 195). Validity is an incredibly important characteristic to consider when choosing a measurement technique to implement (Siniscalco & Auriat, 2005). For this study, validity refers to the extent to which the hypotheses measure intentions to disclose personal information in the use of IoT. Ajumobi (2014) states that there are specific validity tests for measurement procedures and separate validity tests for hypothesis/propositions testing procedures. Several assessments were conducted to ensure convergent and discriminant validities. The average variance extracted (AVE) and composite reliabilities (CR) can be examined for convergent validity, which should be higher than the recommended value of 0.5 (Wang et al., 2016), while Fornell-Larcker Criterion and Hetrotrait-Monotrait (HTMT) ratio of correlations can be conducted to ensure discriminant validity (Hair et al., 2017).

3.5.3. Data Collection

The data collection process occurred once the research design was approved and research instrument received ethical clearance and been tested. Online questionnaires were created using Qualtrics and distributed through email and social media (such as Facebook, Twitter and

Instagram), to ensure that the questionnaire reached as many potential respondents as possible and to eliminate time and cost constraints. Each questionnaire had the following documents attached to it: a cover letter (see **Appendix C**), including an introduction to the study and researcher, co-signed by the supervisor of this study and a participant consent form. The questionnaire was distributed over social media (Facebook, Instagram, LinkedIn), through an anonymous link created on Qualtrics. The following steps were carried out to distribute the questionnaire to potential respondents:

1. A new project was created in Qualtrics, which enabled different questionnaire features.
2. Multiple choice and 5-point Likert scale questions were established as the main method of extrapolating responses, due to the nature of the questions.
3. Validation was added to questions relating to age and current location, as the study focused on people over the age of 18 and those currently living in SA.
4. The research added validation to the questionnaire to ensure that all questions were answered.
5. Validation was added so that the same individual could only answer the questionnaire once.
6. The UCT framework was incorporated, so that respondents were aware that the questionnaire was associated with university research.
7. The researcher changed the look and feel of the survey to improve ease of use for the respondent.
8. The questionnaire was then distributed through various social media platforms through the use of the anonymous link provided by the "distribution" tab, within Qualtrics.

3.6. Data Analysis Techniques

3.6.1. Quantitative:

The data gathered in this study was analysed primarily through quantitative measures and techniques because of the quantitative nature of the research instrument. The data collected through Qualtrics needed to be cleaned to remove potential anomalies, which was done using Microsoft Excel. The data cleaning process involved a rigorous analysis to reveal any invalid or incomplete data, the processes includes the need to ensure that all data is correctly filled in and that the data falls within the same range on the Likert scale. Once the data was cleaned, the data was coded into numbers based on the scaling stated in section 3.5 (e.g. 1 – 5), thereafter, the excel data was exported into a csv. file, as SmartPLS can only import csv. and txt. files. This research adopted the Partial Least Squares (PLS) - Structural Equation Modelling (SEM) method for data analysis purposes, PLS provides the best fit compared with other SEM techniques (Kim et al., 2019). SEM is a non-parametric data analysis method, which is adopted when analysing data that does not require data to meet particular distributional assumptions, through the use of R values, path coefficients, hypotheses testing and several other statistical measures (Hair et al., 2017; Sanchez, 2013). The method supports positivistic research (Hair et al., 2017), which focuses on assessing the significance between dependent and multiple independent variables (Sanchez, 2013), hence it being appropriate for this research.

3.7. Limitations

Through the adoption of a survey strategy and the combination of a questionnaire, there is a limit to the number of questions that can be asked (Saunders et al., 2009), without becoming overbearing on the respondents, therefore knowledge gained can be regarded as limited to isolated points, which may not illustrate findings that will hold over a constant period of time. Questionnaires provide outcomes related to trends and attitudes but are not able to fully investigate and provide reasons for those outcomes (Beiske, 2002). Although a survey strategy is able to elicit information about factors relating to attitudes and perceptions, which is difficult to measure through a more observational approach, the strategy merely provides estimates rather than exact measurements (Glasow, 2005).

3.8. Ethics and Confidentiality

Ethics within research refers to the use of moral values when conducting, analysing and communicating outcomes of a study (Myers, 2013). The researcher acknowledged the need for integrity and moral values within research (Bhattacherjee, 2012; Saunders et al., 2009). Therefore, the research instrument incorporated within this study, was first sent to the ethics committee at the University of Cape Town (UCT) for review, along with ethical application forms. Once ethical clearance was received, the data collection process began, whereby the questionnaire (see Appendix B) was complemented with a cover letter (see Appendix A), detailing the purpose of the study and that completing the questionnaire was considered a voluntary act. All participants in this study were ensured that their responses were treated with anonymity, although demographical information such as age and gender were collected and used in an attempt to accomplish stipulated research objectives. The raw data collected was considered confidential, with only the researcher having possession and access to it. All the information and data collected within this study, were kept on the researcher's personal computer, which was protected by a password, while a backup was stored on the researcher's cloud storage (One Drive), safeguarded through the use of another password. This protective structure was maintained throughout the research process.

3.9. Time Frame

This study adopted a cross-sectional timeframe due to time constraints and the nature and aim of the study. Saunders et al. (2009) explains that a study must be considered cross-sectional when the proposed study is orientated around gaining an understanding of a present phenomenon (or phenomena) within a particular timeframe, whereby a one-year time period is mentioned. The cross-sectional timeframe was appropriate because of the amount of time the university affords a student to complete the Masters' programme. The timeframe was aligned with best practice with regards to survey studies (Saunders et al., 2009). Below is a break-down of the various deliverable completion dates.

Deliverable	Due Date
Research Design, Literature and Research Design Deliverables	2017
Pilot Testing	2018
Data Collection	2018
Hiatus and supervisor change	
Data Analysis	2019
Write up of findings and conclusions	2019
Editing	2019-2020
Final submission of the book	2020

Table 3: Research Time Frame.

3.10. Research Design Summary

The objective of this research was to understand the cause of the Privacy Paradox, by identifying factors that influence information disclosure in the use of IoT. This chapter has provided an overview of the research design and methodology adopted within this study;

establishing the philosophical stance chosen, which subsequently influences the research approaches, methods and techniques that were used. Table 4 depicts a summary of the research methodology for this study.

Methodology	Approach
Philosophy	Positivist
Research Strategy	Survey
Research Purpose	Explanatory research
Research Approach	Deductive
Target Population	IoT users in SA above the age of 18
Type of research	Quantitative research
Data Collection Techniques	Questionnaire
Data Analysis	Quantitative: • Qualtrics • Microsoft Excel • SmartPLS 3
Timeframe	Cross-sectional

Table 4: Research Design Summary.

4. Research Analysis, Findings and Discussion

4.1. Introduction

To achieve the purpose of this research, an online survey instrument was constructed and administered to IoT users within SA. As previously established in section 3.4.2, a meaningful sample size of 385 or greater was required to achieve a 95% confidence level (Qualtrics, 2019). A total of 507 questionnaire responses were received. **395** responses were found to be valid, with 112 (of the 507) responses removed during the analysis phase due to the following reasons:

- Prior to the questionnaire being distributed to the general public/considered active, it had initially been pushed through the pilot study phase, during that phase it became prevalent that some respondents failed to answer all the questions before submitting. After the pilot study phase, settings were added to ensure that respondents knew they had to answer all the questions before submitting. Any uncompleted questionnaires would be deemed unacceptable for data analysis and subsequently removed from the study.

- During the initial process of the data analysis process all responses' standard deviation were analysed. Any response with a standard deviation of 0 was removed because a standard deviation of 0 illustrates that a respondent selected the same answer for every question, which indicates that a respondent was not engaged with the questionnaire (Bhattacherjee, 2012; Hellerstein, 2008).

This section initially discusses various demographic information of the 395 participants that was extrapolated from the results obtained. Subsequently, the researcher incorporated Smart PLS 3 to construct and analyse the initial model through the complete bootstrapping method. The model was tested through the use of rigorous statistical methods such as reliability and validity tests, thereafter a revaluation of the model took place to conform to statistical standards. Once a suitable model was established and regarded as a "good fit" for this study, through tests conducted on both the outer and inner models; hypotheses testing was carried out.

4.2. Demographic Analysis

The following section relates to demographic data collected within this study.

4.2.1. Gender

As illustrated below in figure 6, the sample consisted of 395 valid responses which was split 24,05% (n=95) male; 75,44% (n=298) female and 0.005% (n=2) identified themselves as "other". This comes as a surprise, as research indicates that between the ages of 18-29 (see figure 7) there is an even split between male and female interaction over social media (one of the distribution mediums for the online questionnaire) within SA (Statista, 2020). However, Smith's (2008) research illustrated that data gathered from online surveys, can be considered free of gender bias and won't distort overall findings.

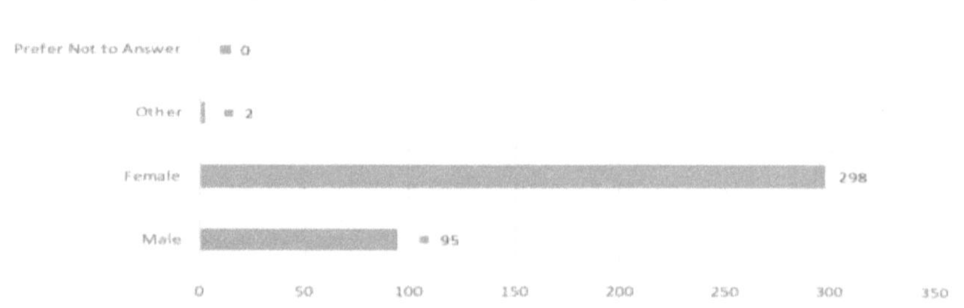

Figure 6: Gender Distribution.

4.2.2. Age of Respondents

According to figure 7, the age distribution was positively skewed with majority of respondents being between the ages of 18 and 29 years old (n=345), followed by respondents between the ages of 30-39 years old (n=38). The remaining respondents (n=12) were above the age of 40, the questionnaire had validation inserted to not allow individuals that stated they were below the age of 18 to answer it. This is in line with current statistics which postulates that majority of social media users within SA are between the ages of 18-34 (Statista, 2020).

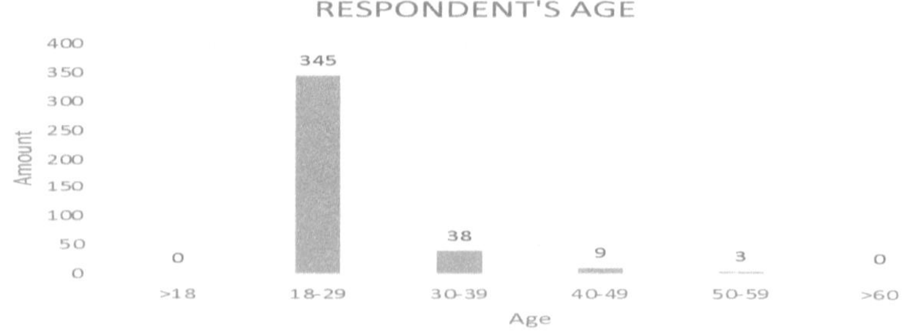

Figure 7: Age Distribution

4.2.3. Education

Based on figure 8, majority of the respondents' highest current qualification was a high school certificate (n=164), followed by a university undergraduate qualification (n=109), thereafter a university postgraduate qualification (n=77). Due to the age demographic in which the majority of respondents were between the 18-29, the number of individuals with a minimum high school certificate qualification correlates with the rising statistic of individuals matriculating and going on to pursue tertiary/vocational education post-apartheid (Macha & Kadakia, 2017).

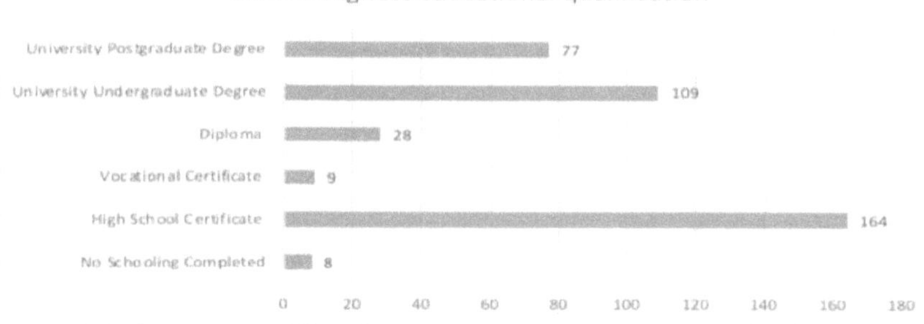

Figure 8: Highest Current Educational Qualification.

4.2.4.   Have individuals heard of the term "Internet of Things (IoT)", prior to this study?

Based on figure 9, majority of the respondents had not heard of the term IoT prior to being involved in this study, with 70% (n=275) stating that they hadn't heard of it before and the remaining 30% (n=120) stipulating that they had heard of it before.

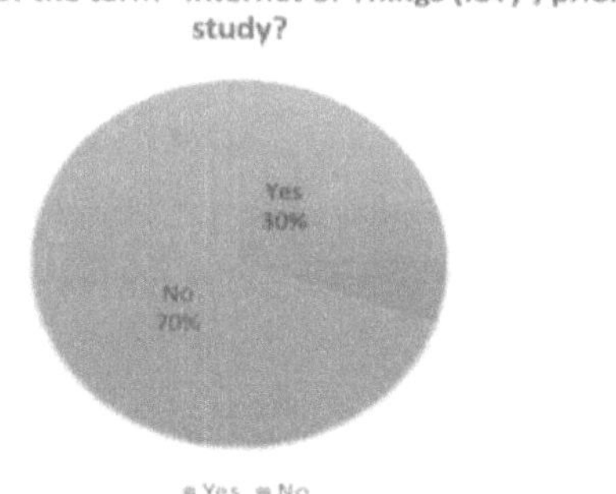

Figure 9: Aware of the Term IoT before this Study

4.2.5.   How often do you use IoT devices and applications?

According to figure 10, majority of respondents stated that they used IoT "a great deal" (n=258) throughout their daily lives, followed by smaller portions of the responsive pool stating that they use IoT "a lot" (n=95) and a moderate amount (n=34), with the remaining going on to stating that they use IoT a little (n=8) or not at all (n=0). This means that people in SA are spending a particularly large amount of their time interacting with IoT in one form or another, which is indicative of the strides the country particularly, the city of Cape Town is making to become more technologically averse (Lourie, 2017).

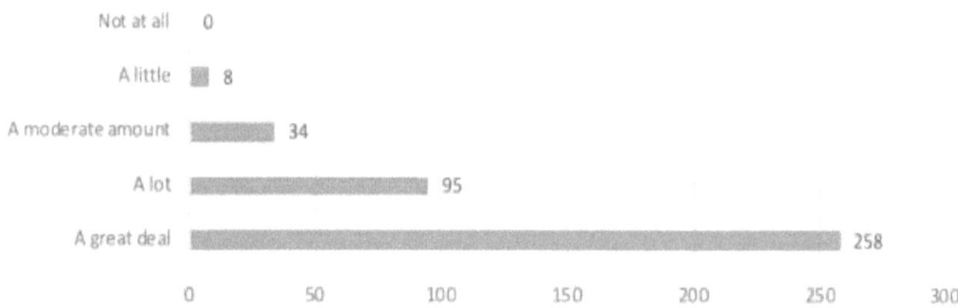

Figure 10: IoT Frequency of Use.

4.2.6.   In what instance are you most likely to use IoT devices?

With a view on the data collected, figure 11 illustrates what respondents predominately use IoT for. 230 Respondents stated that they spend the majority of the time using IoT for leisure purposes (n=58%), with 137 respondents indicating that they used IoT for work-related matters (n=35%), while 15 respondents indicated that they mostly use IoT for other matters (n=4%) and the remaining 13 respondents use IoT for fitness related matters (n=3%). This correlates with previous literature indicating that besides cameras and innocuous nodes, smartphones, tablets and smart TVs form part of the most used IoT devices (Sinha, 2017; Williams et al., 2017).

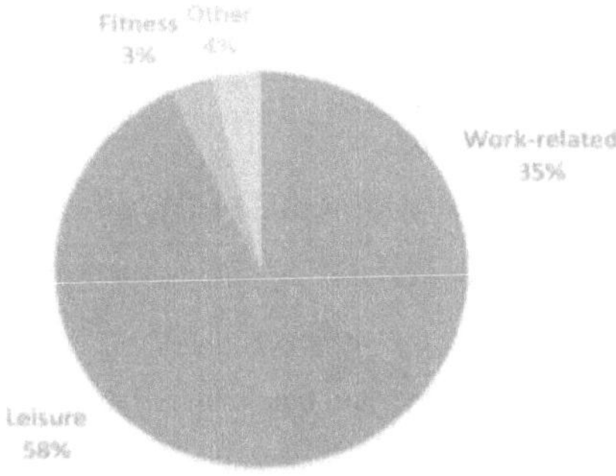

Figure 11: Instances of Usage

4.2.7. *Summary of Demographic Analysis*

In summary, the above statistics indicated that bulk of the respondents identified themselves as female (n= 298), with the majority of respondents being between the age of eighteen and twenty-nine, 350 of the respondents had at least completed high school, with a further 53% of those respondents having completed tertiary education. 70% of the respondents we not aware of the term IoT before this study, while majority of the respondents indicated that they used IoT "a great deal" in their daily lives, which was particularly used for leisure purposes.

4.3. Statistical Analysis through Smart PLS 3 – Initial Model

Within the IS stream of research, the SEM modelling method has been often used for data analysis to evaluate the difference in variance between dependent and independent variables (Hair et al., 2017; Rönkkö, McIntosh, Antonakis, & Edwards, 2016). Within this study, the complete bootstrapping procedure in Smart PLS 3 was used, to test statistical significance of the data sets (Hair et al., 2017). Rönkkö et al. (2016) explains that in complete bootstrapping, the original set of data is randomly observed as sub-samples to estimate the PLS path model. The process consists of randomly drawing sub-samples from the data set until a large number of sub-samples is created and observed to determine PLS-SEM results (Hair et al. 2014; Hair et al. 2017). Subsequently the significance of PLS-SEM results were assessed through evaluating the populated p-values, t-values and confidence intervals from the subsamples bootstrapping process (Hair et al., 2017).

4.3.1. Procedure within SmartPLS:

1. The research model developed within this study, as well as the associated cleaned data were populated into Smart PLS. Thereafter, associations between the constructs and data were implemented.

2. Once the model was digitally structured within the Smart PLS, several statistical tests were run to assess both the inner and outer models. Some of these tests related to validity and reliability tests within the outer model, as well as the Coefficient of Determination (r^2) and the model's goodness of fit tests within the inner model.

3. Thirdly, to determine which factors influence information disclosure in the use of IoT in SA, hypotheses testing and path coefficient tests were conducted; to confirm whether the hypotheses established earlier within this study were valid.

Figure 12 illustrates the initial model in Smart PLS developed from point 1 in the abovementioned process (Hair et al., 2014). Figure 12 illustrates the outer loadings which provides an indication on which independent variables provide the highest degree of influence on their associated dependent variable (construct).

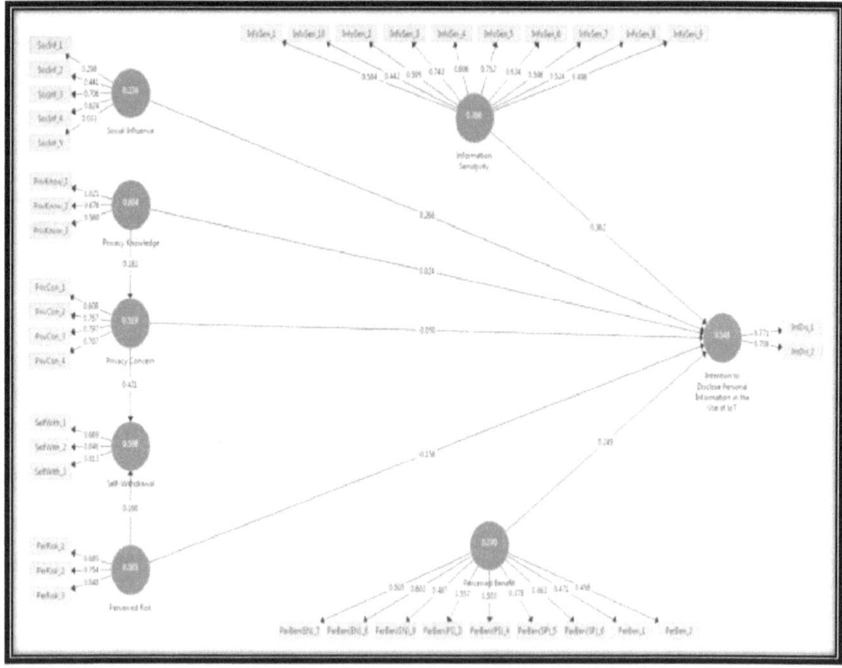

Figure 12: Initial Conceptual Model in SmartPLS.

The relationship between independent variables and their measuring items (constructs) were defined as the outer model. The outer model was evaluated through the following reliability and validity tests: Internal Consistency Reliability Testing, Construct Reliability, Convergent Validity Test and Discriminant Validity Test. The aforementioned tests were suggested by previous studies as valid tests within quantitative research for evaluating the outer model (Byrne, 2013; Hair et al., 2017). Therefore, the following tests were conducted to deduce the outer model findings (Hair, Sarstedt, Hopkins & Kuppelwieser, 2014):

- Internal Consistency Reliability Testing
- Construct Reliability
- Convergent Validity Test
- Discriminant Validity Test

4.4.1.   Reliability and Validity Testing

4.4.1.1.   Internal Consistency Reliability Testing

The internal consistency tests attempt to explain how well each question within a research instrument represents its respective variable/construct (Hair et al., 2014). Internal consistency reliability tests within this study focused on observing the Cronbach's Alpha and Dillon-Goldstein's (rho_A) values, after running a complete bootstrapping in Smart PLS (Alexandrou & Chen, 2014; Hair et al., 2017). A complete bootstrapping is a nonparametric statistical analysis procedure that is used to test the significance of path coefficients by observing R^2 values, rho_A, Cronbach's alpha, and other resulting values in Smart PLS (Hair et al., 2017). Cronbach's Alpha values are normally deemed acceptable at a threshold of 0.70; however, a threshold of 0.60 can be considered sufficient (Fornell & Larcker, 1981; Hair et al., 2006). "Dillon-Goldstein's rho is a better reliability measure than Cronbach's alpha in SEM, since it is based on the loadings rather than the correlations between the observed variables." (Demo, Neiva, Nunes & Rozzett, 2012, p.402). Hair et al. (2017) goes on to explain that an acceptable rho_A value is above or equal to 0.7.

Variables	No of items measured	Cronbach's Alpha	Dillion-Goldstein's (rho_A)
Information Sensitivity	10	0.84	0.86
Privacy Concern	4	0.81	0.82
Privacy Knowledge	3	0.80	0.89
Social Influence	5	0.54	0.65
Self-withdrawal	3	0.75	0.77
Perceived Benefits	9	0.77	0.78
Perceived Risks	3	0.80	0.82
Intentions to Disclose	2	0.71	0.71

Table 5: Reliability Test Results.

Table 5 shows the results of the Cronbach's alpha test for each construct. Information Sensitivity had a Cronbach's alpha of 0.84, Privacy Concern had a Cronbach's alpha of 0.81, Privacy Knowledge had a Cronbach's alpha of 0.80, Social Influence had a Cronbach's alpha of 0.54, Perceived Benefits had a Cronbach's alpha of 0.7 and Perceived Risk had a Cronbach's alpha of 0.80. Continuing on that, with the majority of the observed rho_A values ranging between 0.71 and 0.89 for the study, most of the constructs passed the internal consistency reliability test. This indicates that majority of the constructs have high internal consistency and can be considered reliable measures. Social Influence results were lower than what is recommended within literature, therefore a model re-evaluation process will occur in section 4.4.1.2.

4.4.1.2.   Model Re-evaluation

To improve Reliability and Validity, all outer loadings with values between 0.40 and 0.70 can be considered for removal (Hair et al., 2014). **Appendix F** consists of a table providing each item and subsequent outer loading, the process began where outer loadings between 0.4 and 0.7 were removed where necessary to improve Cronbach's Alpha and rho_A values. Below figure 13 represents the re-evaluated model which illustrates the removal of items with associated "weaker" outer loadings illustrated in figure 12, which indicates the higher influence of information sensitivity and perceived benefit on the main dependent variable:

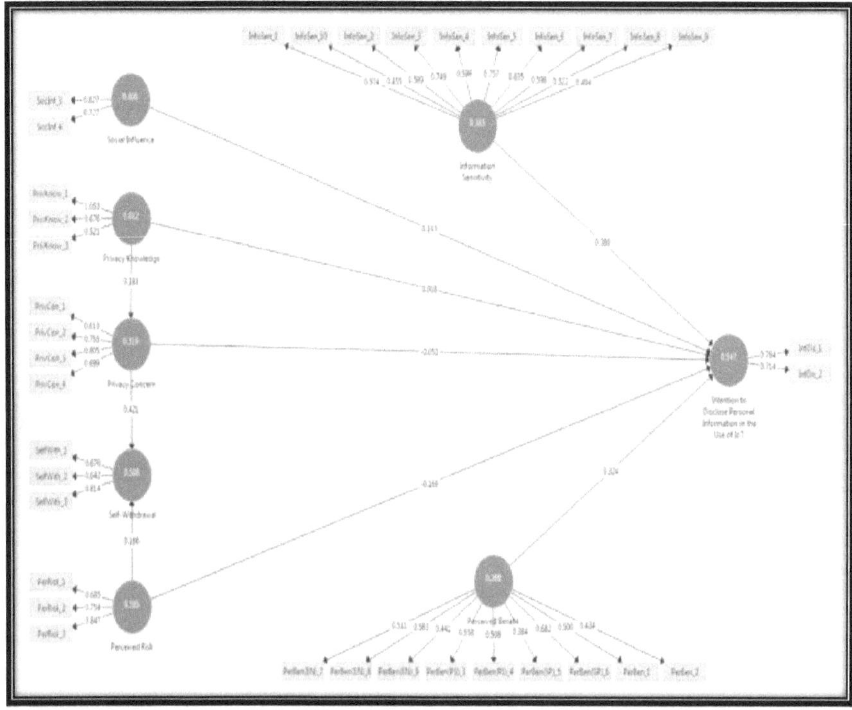

Figure 13: Re-evaluated Model in SmartPLS.

4.4.1.3.   Construct Reliability

The previous section focused on the reliability of constructs in relationship to each other. In this section, the focus is on assessing the relationship between items of each construct to each other and how they are related to items of other constructs, the research incorporated the new Cronbach's Alpha results, as well as a composite reliability test. The Composite Reliability test requires a score of 0.7 (0.6 for exploratory research) to be considered acceptable and for the construct to be considered reliable (Hair, Ringle & Sarstedt, 2014). The difference between Cronbach's Alpha and Composite Reliability test, is that Composite Reliability considers the number of outer loadings that make up each construct resulting in a more accurate evaluation of reliability (Hair et al., 2014). Table 6 reflects that all composite reliability results range from 0.71 to 0.85, indicating that items for each construct truly represent the construct.

Variables	No of items measured	Cronbach's Alpha	Composite Reliability
Information Sensitivity	10	0.84	0.85
Privacy Concern	4	0.81	0.81
Privacy Knowledge	3	0.80	0.81
Social Influence	2	0.75	0.75
Self-withdrawal	3	0.75	0.75
Perceived Benefits	9	0.77	0.76
Perceived Risks	3	0.80	0.81
Intentions to Disclose	2	0.71	0.71

Table 6: Construct Reliability Test Results.

4.4.1.4. Convergent Validity Test

Convergent validity tests illustrate how well the questions posed within the instrument represent each construct are related (Hair et al., 2014). To establish convergent validity, the outer loadings of each construct were measured by the Average Variance Extracted (AVE), in which AVE is recommended to be equal to or greater than 0.5 to establish convergent validity (see table 7) (Wang et al., 2016). AVE, "shows the percentage of variance interpreted by the latent factors from measurement error. The larger the AVE is, the larger indicator variance could be interpreted by the latent variables and the smaller relative measured error is" (Shyu, Li, & Tang, 2013, p. 13).

Construct	Average Variance Extracted (AVE)	Valid?
Information Sensitivity	0.37	No
Privacy Concern	0.52	Yes
Privacy Knowledge	0.61	Yes
Social Influence	0.61	Yes
Self-withdrawal	0.51	Yes
Perceived Benefits	0.27	No

| Perceived Risks | 0.59 | Yes |
| Intentions to Disclose | 0.55 | Yes |

Table 7: Convergent Reliability Test Results.

Based on the above results all Composite Reliability results were deemed acceptable, except for Information Sensitivity and perceived benefits, which were too low and regarded as unacceptable. Prompting a secondary re-evaluation of the outer loadings (Hair et al., 2014), which is illustrated in section 4.4.1.5.

4.4.1.5.   Re-evaluated Convergent Validity Assessment Table

Construct	Average Variance Extracted (AVE)	Valid?
Information Sensitivity	0.41	YES
Privacy Concern	0.52	Yes
Privacy Knowledge	0.61	Yes
Social Influence	0.61	Yes
Self-withdrawal	0.51	Yes
Perceived Benefits	0.41	YES
Perceived Risks	0.59	Yes
Intentions to Disclose	0.55	Yes

Table 8: Re-evaluated Convergent Validity Assessment Results.

"AVE should be higher than 0.5. However, the value of 0.4 is acceptable due to condition that if AVE value is less than 0.5, but composite reliability is higher than 0.6, the convergent validity of the construct is acceptable" (Safiih & Azreen, 2016, p. 46). Huang, Wang, Wu and Wang (2013) concur with this, expressing the rule Fornell and Larcker (1981) declared, in which if AVE is below 0.5 but composite reliability is greater than 0.6 (see table 9 below) then convergent validity of a construct is regarded as satisfactory. Table 9 represents final Cronbach's Alpha, rho_A and Composite Reliability values based on the re-evaluation of the model in relation to the final AVE results.

Variables	Items	Cronbach's Alpha	rho_A	Composite Reliability
Information Sensitivity	9	0.86	0.87	0.86
Privacy Concern	4	0.81	0.82	0.81
Privacy Knowledge	3	0.80	0.90	0.81
Social Influence	2	0.75	0.76	0.76
Self-withdrawal	3	0.75	0.77	0.75
Perceived Benefits	4	0.74	0.74	0.74
Perceived Risks	3	0.80	0.82	0.81
Intentions to Disclose	2	0.71	0.71	0.71

Table 9: Summary table after Re-evaluated model.

4.4.1.6.   Discriminant Validity Test

Discriminant validity is the degree to which different constructs of a model are unrelated (Farrell & Rudd, 2009; Hair et al., 2017). Hair et al. (2014) goes on to explain that the discriminant validity is used to assess if there is truly no relationship on the constructs that are not supposed to be related within a particular model, this ensures that each construct represents a unique factor which affects the dependent construct. Cross-loading assess discriminant validity by expecting items or indicators of a construct to load higher together on their construct than they can do on other constructs or latent variables (Arif, 2016; Hair et al., 2014). A complete bootstrapping was run in SmartPLS, in which the Fornell-Larcker criterion and Hetrotrait-Monotrait (HTMT) ratio of correlations were used to determine discriminant validity.

4.4.1.6.1. Fornell-Larcker Criterion

In the Fornell-Larcker criterion, "a researcher compares the AVE of each construct with the shared variance between constructs" (Farrell & Rudd, 2009, p. 3). For the reflective constructs to be valid, "we test to see if the square root of every AVE value belonging to each latent construct is much larger than any correlation among any pair of latent constructs" (Zait & Bertea, 2011, p. 218). If this is the case, which table 10 postulates, then the results passed the discriminant validity test (Hair et al., 2014; Henseler, Ringle & Sarstedt, 2014).

	Information Sensitivity	Intention to Disclose	Perceived Benefit	Perceived Risk	Privacy Concern	Privacy Knowledge	Self-Withdrawal	Social Influence
Information Sensitivity	0,638							
Intention to Disclose	0,597	0,740						
Perceived Benefit	0,139	0,467	0,642					
Perceived Risk	-0,200	-0,247	0,068	0,766				
Privacy Concern	-0,222	-0,294	-0,151	0,402	0,721			
Privacy Knowledge	0,004	-0,010	0,070	0,068	0,180	0,781		
Self-Withdrawal	-0,007	-0,242	-0,098	0,334	0,487	0,119	0,714	
Social Influence	0,385	0,542	0,441	-0,078	-0,283	-0,182	-0,080	0,780

Table 10: Fornell-Larcker Criterion.

4.4.1.6.2. *Hetrotrait-Monotrait (HTMT) Ratio*

A study carried out by Henseler et al., (2014) explains that the Fornell-Larcker criterion cannot be used as the only measurement metric for discriminant validity, as it has not been able to reliably detect discriminant validity in several other studies. Therefore, the authors propose using the Hetrotrait-Monotrait (HTMT) ratio of correlations, as another method to test discriminant validity (Henseler et al., 2014). HTMT values below 0.9 imply that discriminant validity has been established between to reflective constructs. Based on table 11, the maximum HTMT value is 0.597, this is below 0.90 which is the most conservative HTMT value. Therefore, one can conclude that discriminant validity has been established.

	Information Sensitivity	Intention to Disclose	Perceived Benefit	Perceived Risk	Privacy Concern	Privacy Knowledge	Self-Withdrawal	Social Influence
Information Sensitivity								
Intention to Disclose	0,597							

Perceived Benefit	0,180	0,464						
Perceived Risk	0,205	0,247	0,106					
Privacy Concern	0,227	0,294	0,151	0,402				
Privacy Knowledge	0,093	0,053	0,156	0,094	0,174			
Self-Withdrawal	0,067	0,243	0,137	0,336	0,488	0,124		
Social Influence	0,375	0,538	0,454	0,090	0,288	0,186	0,081	

Table 11: HTMT Values.

The above assessments (internal consistency reliability, construct reliability, convergent validity and discriminant validity assessments), illustrate that the outer model (the relationship between constructs and their items) are considered valid and reliable, since all tests were successful. Therefore, the outer model can be considered statistically significant for this study (Rönkkö et al., 2015).

4.5. Inner Model Assessment Findings

The previous sections focused on assessing the validity of the outer model or the relationship between independent constructs with their items. This section presents the relationship between the dominant dependent construct (intention to disclose personal information in the use of IoT), the minor dependent constructs (privacy concern and self-withdrawal) and independent constructs (perceived risk, perceived benefit, social influence, privacy knowledge and information sensitivity) of the conceptual model defined in section 2.16. Within the conceptual model, the relationship between the dependent construct and independent constructs are defined as the inner model. The inner model assessments enable researchers to answer their research questions through hypotheses testing (Arif, 2016; Hair et al., 2014). The following tests were run with regards to inner model assessments; the coefficient of determination, path coefficient and model goodness of fit (Hair et al., 2017). The following tests were conducted to deduce the outer model findings (Hair et al., 2014; Hair et al., 2017):

- The Coefficient of Determination (r^2)
- The Model's Goodness of Fit
- Hypothesis Testing and Path Coefficients

4.5.1. The Coefficient of Determination (r^2)

Hair et al. (2017) stipulate that the coefficient of determination evaluation is a measure which is used in research to evaluate the conceptual model's hypothesised relationships. The coefficient of determination (R^2) predicts the variability in one latent variable and how the variation of a different latent variable can explain it (Hair et al., 2014). The closer the R^2 is to 1, the more accurate the constructs can predict variability (Hair et al., 2017). Table 12 illustrates the R^2 values, after running a complete bootstrapping in SmartPLS.

Dependent Variable	Coefficient of Determination (R^2)
Intention to Disclose Personal Information in the Use of IoT	0.593
Privacy Concern	0.032
Self-withdrawal	0.260

Table 12: Coefficients of Determination.

- Observed coefficient of determination was 0.593 for the relationship between the dependent construct (intention to disclose personal information in the use of IoT) and independent construct (perceived risk, perceived benefit, social influence, privacy knowledge and information sensitivity).

- According to table 12, the model has satisfactory predictive accuracy when it comes to predicting prospective outcomes (Cangur & Erca, 2015; Hair et al., 2014). Therefore, the inner model is considered valid based on R^2, which indicates significance between the dependent construct and the independent constructs. The dependent construct proved to be predictable from the independent constructs, according to the results.

4.5.2. The Model's Goodness of Fit

The goodness of fit test was conducted to assess the inner model's best fit, to measure model fit the Standardised Root Mean Square Residual (SRMR) was observed to assess the discrepancies between expected correlations and observed correlations as an average (Hair et al., 2017; Henseler et al., 2014). SRMR values of 0.08 and less defines a good fit for the model (Hair et al., 2017; Henseler et al., 2014; Cangur & Ercan, 2015). Table 13 shows the results of the SmartPLS PLS Algorithm test for goodness of fit test.

Test Observed	Saturated Model
SRMR	0.064

Table 13: SRMR Results.

The observed results for the conceptual model were represented as the saturated model, which implies the usage of data from the original conceptual model (Figure 12). The observed SRMR after running the PLS Algorithm bootstrapping was 0.064, which is below the recommended 0.08 (Hair et al., 2017). The results observed from the SRMR goodness of fit test suggested that data used for the study fitted well to the conceptual model of the study.

4.6. Hypothesis Testing and Path Coefficients

To address the research questions within this study, research stipulates that hypothesis testing and path coefficient analysis should be performed (Roky & Al-Meriouh, 2015). Therefore, the relationship between the dependent construct and independent constructs was hypothesised using constructs from previous studies associated to the privacy paradox within the IS domain: Information Sensitivity (Marwick & Hargittai, 2018; von Entreß-Fürsteneck, Buchwald, & Urbach, 2019), Privacy Concern (Hallam & Zanella, 2016; Libaque-Saenz et al., 2016; Williams et al., 2017); Self-withdrawal (Dienlin & Metzger, 2016), Perceived Risk (Castro & Bettencourt, 2017; Cheung et al., 2015), Perceived Benefit (Carignani & Gemmo, 2018; Yoo, Hand & Huang,), Social Influence (Hein, Jodoin, Rauschnabel & Ivens, 2018; Wang, Meister, & Gray, 2013), Privacy Knowledge (Barth et al., 2019; Belanger & Crossler, 2019; Taddicken, 2014) and Intentions to Disclose Information in the use of IoT (Beuker, 2016). Additionaly. The relationship between latent constructs were defined as **paths** and the measure of significance of latent constructs' relationship were defined as the **path coefficient** (Cangur & Ercan, 2015).

To determine the factors influencing information disclosure in the use of the IoT in SA a significance test was performed between each variable. A 500 resamples (complete) bootstrapping method was conducted to test for significance (Kim et al., 2019). Table 14 outlines the results from performing the significance test, in which the level of significance is represented by the p-value. The p-value shows the probability of observing the null hypotheses (Hair et al., 2014), therefore, a significance level of less than 0.05 is recommended, to ensure a low probability of observing the null hypothesis. A high p-value (p > 0.05) suggests that the data collected does not provide sufficient evidence to accept the hypothesis. Table 14 illustrates the t-value as well, where the smaller the magnitude of the t-value, the greater the evidence to reject the hypothesis (Hair et al., 2014).

With that in mind, previous literature postulates that path coefficients that exceed than 0.2 are considered significant for quantitative research data analysis (Cangur & Ercan, 2015). Another indicator of good significance is achieved whereby t-values are above 1.95, while corresponding p-values are less than 0.05 (Hair et al., 2014; Roky & Al-Meriouh, 2015). Roky and Al-Meriouh (2015) go on to elaborate that high significance is achieved when p-values that are less than or equal to 0.001, have corresponding t-values that are greater than 3.29.

Note: NS = Not Significant. NS: p > 0.05 | ** p < 0.05 | *** p < 0.01

	Relationship	Path Coefficient	T-Value	P-Value	Level of Significance	Outcome?
H1	Information Sensitivity -> Intentions to disclose information in the use of IoT	0.431	6.802	<0.000001	***	Supported
H2	Privacy Concern -> Intentions to disclose information in the use of IoT	-0.031	0.471	0.638166	NS	Not Supported
H3	Perceived Risk -> Intentions to disclose information in the use of IoT	-0.154	2.427	0.015574	**	Supported
H4	Perceived Benefits -> Intentions to disclose information in the use of IoT	0.315	4.504	0.000008	***	Supported
H5	Social Influence -> Intentions to disclose information in the use of IoT	0.220	2.478	0.013528	**	Supported
H6	Privacy Knowledge -> Privacy Concern	0.180	3.054	0.002376	***	Supported
H7	Privacy Knowledge -> Intentions to disclose information in the use of IoT	0.022	0.366	0.714752	NS	Not Supported
H8	Privacy Concern -> Self-Withdrawal	0.421	5.638	<0.000001	***	Supported
H9	Perceived Risk -> Self-Withdrawal	0.165	2.093	0.036824	**	Supported

Table 14: Significant Testing Results (Hypotheses Testing).

SEM was used to test the relationship between latent constructs (Byrne, 2013). This study assessed the hypotheses formulated in section 2.14 and the relationships of constructs within the inner model assessment and path coefficients were observed after running a complete bootstrapping analysis in Smart PLS 3 (Hair et al., 2017). Based on table 14, two relationships within the model are considered "not supported", the results of the hypotheses testing are discussed in section 4.8.

4.7. Findings

The following section documents and discusses the findings that were extrapolated from the research analysis section, in which the above hypotheses testing was done to answer the research questions mentioned in section 1.2.2. The Cronbach's alpha, rho_A and composite reliability values indicated that all constructs have high internal consistency, so one can assume that the constructs effectively measured intention to disclose personal information in the use of IoT (Hair et al. 2014).

4.7.1. Hypotheses

4.7.1.1. Information Sensitivity

This study considered **information sensitivity** in the following context, Prince (2018) stated that the type of information plays an important role in disclosure decisions. Doig (2016) agreed by identifying that individuals are willing to provide information when the sensitivity and importance of that information is valued at a low sensitivity; such as gender, age and marital status, while going on to explain that the greater the sensitivity of the information; such as financial records and passwords, the less likely disclosure will occur. "As more personal information is digitalized and shared, the privacy risk of IoT service users increases" (Kim et al., 2019, p.274). The influence of information sensitivity was tested through the following hypothesis:

H1: Information sensitivity influences willingness to disclose personal information.

According to table 14, as well as figure 13, the observed path coefficient for information sensitivity on the intention to disclose personal information in the use of IoT was 0.431, therefore H1 is supported. The results imply that the sensitivity of the information being utilised by IoT has a positive influence on information disclosure, which aligns with the above literature from Doig (2016) and Prince (2018). With a p value of < 0.01 and t-value of > 3.29

(p = <0.000001 and t = 6.802), it can be inferred that information sensitivity has a significant influence on intentions to disclose personal information in the use of IoT. Based on the indicator mean's in Appendix E, individuals were more inclined to disclose descriptive information such as name, surname and e-mail address but were less inclined to disclose financial and health related information, which is in line with previous literature.

4.7.1.2.   Privacy Concern

As mentioned previously in section 2, privacy concern refers to individuals' worries relating to potential loss or misuse of information (Xu, Dinev, Smith & Hart, 2011). Privacy concerns are subjective and contextual, that vary based on an individual's personal characteristics, understanding and past experiences (Libaque-Saenz et al., 2016). Libaque-Saenz et al. (2016) go on to state that individuals' privacy concerns will vary, and those concerns will subsequently influence their behavioural beliefs and decisions. Kisekka et al. (2013) and Ortiz, Chih and Tsai (2018) posit that an individual privacy concerns negatively influence self-disclosure and that an individual's overall attitudes towards privacy influence their disclosure behaviour. In contrast, some research (Kehr et al., 2015; Taddei & Contena, 2013; Taddicken, 2014), found that there is little to no relationship between privacy concerns and information disclosure, hence the privacy paradox exists (Beuker, 2016). Therefore, the following hypotheses was developed:

H2: Privacy concerns influences individuals' willingness to disclose personal information.

Based on the abovementioned tests, H2 was not supported. According to Appendix E, the indicator means for PrivCon indicate that individuals are concerned about their personal information in the use of IoT. A path coefficient value of -0.031 was observed in section 4.6, which is regard as low, while results (p > 0.05 and t-value of 0.471) implies that the relationship between privacy concern and intention to disclose personal information in the use of IoT was insignificant. Therefore, this research agrees with Beuker (2016) findings, in which privacy concern does not influence intentions to disclose personal information in the use of IoT.

4.7.1.3.   Perceived Risk

Perceived risks relate to information privacy concerns, such as unauthorised collecting and sharing of individuals' personal information (Hajli & Lin, 2016; Myerscough, Lowe & Alpert,

2008). Literature emphasises that individuals exhibit great concern over the way in which organisations elicit unethical procedures with the aim of collecting and using personal information, without consent of those involved (Aleisa & Renaud, 2017a; Keith et al., 2013). Privacy risk perceptions in relation to technology are considered a significant determinant in reduced intentions to disclose (Keith et al., 2013; Wang et al., 2016).

H3: Perceived privacy risk negatively influences the willingness to provide personal information.

Based on what was previously mentioned by H3, the relationship between perceived risk and self-withdrawal was considered significant. Although literature postulates that the influence that perceived risk has on intention to disclose, is equally as high, which this study agrees with. The path coefficient (-0.154) indicates the negative influence perceived risk has on one's intention to disclose information in the use of IoT, while (p = 0.015574 and t = 2.427) emphasis the significance of the relationship between the independent and dependent variable.

4.7.1.4.   *Perceived Benefit*

"Following the economic view of privacy as a commodity, people trade privacy to accrue benefits." (Hallam & Zanella, 2017, p.218). This belief has been expressed several times within the literature review (Crossler & Bélanger, 2017; Jiang et al., 2013; Krasnova et al., 2010; Xu et al., 2011; Wang et al., 2016). Hypothesis 5 incorporates 3 key factors:

- ***Personalised services*** involve organisations augmenting and creating bespoke services that cater an individuals' needs or devices, based upon the information they disclose (Wang et al., 2016).
- ***Self-presentation*** refers to the behaviour of individuals to purposively manage their personal image to other individuals (Wang et al., 2016). Ng's (2014) research revealed that there exists a positive relationship between self-presentation and personal information disclosure.
- Research stipulates that ***enjoyment*** is one of the main components of extrinsic and intrinsic benefits, subsequently making it a pivotal driver of self-disclosure (Dincelli & Zhou, 2017; Krasnova et al., 2010; Yang et al., 2016). The role of enjoyment plays a significant role in self disclosure, as individuals attempt to build relationships through

online interactions and to seek entertainment through virtual services and products (Krasnova, Veltri & Günther, 2012).

H4: *The more people expect benefits by using IoT, the higher their willingness to provide personal information.*

Based on the means within this construct (**Appendix E**), individuals believe using IoT is beneficial and that the pursuit of enjoyment is the driving factor behind disclosing information in the use of IoT. This coincides with 58% of users indicating that they use IoT for leisure purposes. In relation to significance testing (p = 0.000008 and t = 4.504), the influence of perceived benefits on intention to disclose personal information is regarded as significantly high (Hair et al., 2014; Roky & Al-Meriouh, 2015). Therefore, H4 is supported within this study. Enjoyment was the only factor considered in the final model, due to personalised service and self-presentation variables being removed due to the convergent validity results.

4.7.1.5.   Social Influence

Social influence plays a significant role in people's behaviours and how they act (Aljallad, Guo, Chouhan, LaPerriere, Kropczynski, Wisnewski, & Lipford, 2019). When people are put in new or uncertain situations, they often seek advice on how to act, from their social groups (Aljallad et al., 2019). Social influence has been documented as a driver for increased privacy awareness and behaviour and can subsequently make individuals adopt privacy features, which can be shared within their social groups (Mendel & Toch, 2017). Research conducted within the IS sphere, has posited that social influence can significantly influence individual's behaviour (Zhou & Li, 2014). Cheung et al. (2015) stated that both, perceived benefits and social influence positively influence information disclosure.

H5: *Social influence positively influences willingness to disclose personal information.*

The social influence factor's relationship emphasises that H5 is supported. The extrapolated path coefficient value of 0.220 aligns with Cangur and Ercan's (2015) statement that path coefficients greater or equal to 0.20 can be considered highly significant. This is further emphasised by the (p = 0.013528 and t = 2.478) values, which all conform to highly significant standards (Hair et al., 2014; Roky & Al-Meriouh, 2015). The re-evaluated model's outer loadings in Appendix G, indicate that individuals were more comfortable using devices, applications and disclosing information, if their friends and family; were doing so.

4.7.1.6. *Privacy Knowledge*

The importance of perceived ability and knowledge in the context of upholding privacy, cannot be overstated (Crossler & Bélanger, 2017). Do individuals actually know that IoT devices quietly and continuously accumulate their personal data? (Aleisa & Renaud, 2017b). Privacy decisions are constrained by incomplete information and a lack of required knowledge (Kokolakis, 2017; Vitak et al., 2018; Wu, Zhang, Cui & Wang, 2018). The privacy paradox relates to the concern individuals hold about their information but not necessarily upholding corresponding behaviour (Taddicken, 2014). Taddicken (2014) goes on to state that there are various reasons for this, including a lack of problem or risk awareness, a lack of knowledge about protection protocols and a lack of knowledge about what actuals happens to personal information, once revealed. Hence, the more knowledgeable an individual is about privacy and security, the more motivated they are able to be around engaging in privacy averse behaviour (Crossler & Belanger, 2017). This is because an individual will be knowledgeable about potential risks (Crossler & Belanger).

H6: Privacy Knowledge influences Privacy Concern.

H7: Privacy knowledge influences information disclosure.

The observed (p = 0.002376 and t = 3.054) implies that H6 is supported, which is in line with literature. The results indicate that privacy knowledge has a positive influence on privacy concern. The resultant path coefficient of 0.022 implies that H7 is not supported, this is emphasised by the (p = 0.714752 and t = 0.366), therefore privacy knowledge does not influence information disclosure. H7 contradicts Stajkovic and Luthans (1998) in which the authors stated that individuals that consider themselves to have a high level of privacy and security knowledge, exude a stronger conviction to safeguarding their privacy. Chen and Chen (2015) emphasise that, that overconfidence can lead to people becoming less concerned about risks, which subsequently leads to a leniency towards disclosure, which H7 postulates. Therefore, privacy knowledge is not a significant determinant of disclosure.

4.7.1.7. *Self-withdrawal*

The Communication Privacy Management theory (CPM) posits that disclosure and withdrawal are in dialectical tension with each other, meaning that individuals feel competing needs to be both social and private in a privacy context, where 'social' refers to disclosing information and 'private' refers to withholding information (Dienlin & Metzger, 2016). Individuals refrain to disclose information when the security of their data may be compromised, as a result of increased privacy concern (Adelmeyer et al., 2019). Self-withdrawal is employed to avoid negative outcomes and possible risk of communication and disclosure, therefore, being an act of self-protection (Dienlin & Metzger, 2016).

H8: The more concerned people are regarding their privacy, the more they will engage in acts of self-withdrawal.
H9: The more people expect risk in the use of IoT, the more likely people will engage in acts of self-withdrawal.

Although analysis determined that H2 was not supported, the relationship between privacy concern and self-withdrawal appears to be highly significant ($p < 0.001$ and $t = 5.638$), which is illustrated by Adelmeyer et al., (2019), in which the higher concern individuals may have over their information, the more likely those individuals are to engage in self-withdrawal tendencies. Therefore, H8 is supported, Dienlin and Metzger (2016) findings were replicated in this study, with H9 being supported as well. Individuals are more likely to engage in self-withdrawal acts when their privacy is at risk, and the possibility of experiencing negative outcomes become more probable. This is implied by the relationship between perceived risk and self-withdrawal, in which ($p = 0.036824$ and $t = 2.093$).

4.8.   Discussion

Privacy concern and privacy knowledge were factors that had unsupported hypotheses in relation to intention to disclose personal information in the use of IoT. Information sensitivity, perceived risk, perceived benefit and social influence were factors that had supported hypotheses in relation to intention to disclose personal information in the use of IoT. Privacy knowledge however, had supported hypothesis in relation to its influence on privacy concern, while perceived risk and privacy concern had supported hypotheses when it came to the factors' influence on self-withdrawal, which is a counteractive tendency to intention to disclose. Privacy concern's influence has continuously been a contentious topic throughout the literature reviewed. With section 2 (literature review) and section 4 (data analysis) of this study in mind, it becomes apparent that the privacy paradox exists within SA for individuals that use IoT; individuals have expressed that they are concerned about their privacy but have declared their intention to disclose their information in the pursuit of possible benefits such as enjoyment, despite potential risk.

Individuals are more comfortable with revealing less sensitive information, such as their name, date of birth and e-mail address but are more hesitant with their financial, geographical and medical information, which may limit personalised service being fully experienced. Individuals have indicated that they present less than sufficient knowledge around protecting their privacy through the settings of their IoT device(s), nor do they fully know where their data is stored by the manufacturers of the device(s) or what that information is being used for. Based on the findings that this study postulates; it is clear that the IoT is playing a significant role within South African society, specifically for leisure purposes and with a growing influence in industry, which correlates with literature mentioned in section 2. The hesitancy towards revealing pertinent information may indicate society is becoming more security conscious. Although, with perceived benefits in mind and literature illustrating that SA experiences the third highest number of internet-based crimes in the world, that notion may be considered incorrect. Another finding relates to the significance of social influence in the use of applications, technologies and the adoption of security practices. This research documents similar findings of social influence in the use of IoT as that of previous privacy research orientated around SNS, which illustrates the growing and consistent influence social groupings have on individuals.

Although privacy concern does not have a significant influence on information disclosure, this research identified that individuals perceive that there is a high possibility that by using IoT, their information may be misused and that they could run into unexpected problems, which could put their information in jeopardy hence the significant relationship between perceived concern, perceived risk and self-withdrawal. In the context of IoT, based on the path coefficients between perceived risk, perceived benefit and intention to disclose in the use of IoT, as well as the mean responses to PerBen_1, IntDis_1 and IntDis_2; respondents conduct a benefit-risk analysis. With that in mind, benefit has the greater influence on information disclosure, while perceived risk is highly influential when it comes to self-withdrawal. This would confirm that the privacy calculus holds true even in the case of IoT, where the greater the benefit, specifically enjoyment, the more likely information disclosure will occur, knowingly or unknowingly.

5. Conclusion, Limitations and Recommendations

5.1. Conclusion

This research focused on identifying factors that influence personal information in the use of IoT in SA. Despite prior studies investigating the privacy paradox in other forms of information systems (Beuker, 2016; Wang et al., 2016; Williams, 2018), the focus on IoT is in its infancy and the presence within SA is currently limited (Williams, et al., 2017). There are a number of variables taken into account when an individual decides on whether to disclose personal information (Wang et al., 2016) because privacy is subjective; with people viewing and using their information differently (Williams, 2018). After surveying the privacy research landscape, this research incorporated the privacy calculus model, which suggests that individuals engage in a risk-benefit analysis when they share their information and that those individuals can inadvertently become complicit in violating their own privacy (Caron et al., 2016; Wang et al., 2016). Hence, perceived benefits and perceived risks were fundamental in formulating the conceptual model and hypotheses for this research. Additional factors that were observed related to information sensitivity, privacy concern, social influence and privacy knowledge, while the act of self-withdrawal was considered as a counteractive tendency to information disclosure.

The research question was split into secondary research questions and based on the data analysis, it was found that individuals mostly use IoT for leisure purposes, while the final conceptual model indicates that individuals seek to pursue enjoyment and social inclusion above all else, despite their concern regarding their privacy. Those to factors playing the most significant role in understanding why individuals disclose personal information in the use of IoT despite growing concerns about data storage and what their data could be used for. Despite literature emphasising the importance of privacy knowledge, this study found that privacy knowledge had an insignificant influence on individuals' intentions to disclose personal information in the use of IoT. The relationship between privacy concern and intention to disclose illustrates the existence of the privacy paradox within the context of IoT in SA, while the potential benefits override potential risk associated with disclosing information in the use of the innocuous technologies. Heightened levels of privacy concern and perceived risk initiate self-withdrawal tendencies amongst individuals; the results from the hypotheses tests illustrated both positive and significant relationships between the independent variables (privacy concern and perceived risk) and the dependent variable (self-withdrawal).

The results show that privacy concern and perceived risk influence self-withdrawal, while privacy knowledge influences privacy concern. Information sensitivity, social influence, perceived risk and perceived benefit influence information disclosure in the use of IoT.

5.1.1. Research Contribution

The findings for the study have both a knowledge gap and a practical contribution. On the knowledge gap, the model can be used to understand the influence of factors that influence intention to use IoT. The practical contribution is that individuals can gauge how these factors influence their intentions to disclose personal information in the use of IoT and subsequently initiate stricter control measures in place to safeguard their personal information. Service providers can instead illicit greater insights into their potential target market through these influential factors and subsequently intensify the way in which they produce and market their services and products to improve their appeal to a wider audience. Therefore, the model can assist both those manufacturing IoT products and services as well at those that make use of it.

5.1.2. Future Research Directions

Future research on the topic can be expanded through the incorporation of qualitative research practices, which assist researchers to explore hidden, interrelated social processes of a research problem, while focusing on uncovering relevant ideas with respondents through subjective interactions (Bhattacherjee, 2012). Bhattacherjee (2012) goes on to stipulate that qualitative research is predominately focused on interpretative research, in which researchers attempt to interpret social reality (Bhattacherjee, 2012), providing explanatory input in regards to why individuals disclose personal information. A significant theme depicted in research relates to the infancy of data governance surrounding IoT (Shepherd et al., 2017). The large volumes of data collected by IoT needs sufficient governance to avoid data being retained by companies for an unnecessary period of time, which could expose companies to over-sharing, loss and theft of consumer data (Shepherd et al., 2017).

SA has begun to address the need for increased protection through the development of the Protection of Personal Information (PoPI) Act which was signed into law in 2013, although the Act is yet to be fully enforced (Botha, Grobler, Hahn, & Eloff, 2017; Scharnick, Gerber, & Futcher, 2016). The PoPI Act principles were developed to correspond with the majority of the current African data protection laws, PoPI presents a set of principles that prescribe the way in which personal information may be processed (Botha et al., 2017). How legislation and policies influence individuals' intention to disclose personal information in the use of IoT, may offer other insights to what has already been presented in this study, as regulatory requirements are growing in importance (Van Vuuren, 2016).

5.2. Limitations

This study is limited to 395 respondents, although the representative sample was set at 385, future research can be extended by the use of a larger sample of participants to improve current insights into the privacy paradox in the context of IoT within SA or another developing country. The measurement of information sensitivity and perceived benefit was validated at a threshold 0.4 for their respected AVE values, if stricter thresholds are put in place, then alternative findings may be attained. The research took a deductive approach to theory. Future research can consider taking an inductive approach or other methods of theory building to gather results for the research topic. Further research, considering conducting a longitudinal study to collect data over time as opposed to one point in time and potentially increasing the number of respondents exponentially.

6. References

Adelmeyer, M., Meier, P., & Teuteberg, F (2019). Security and Privacy of Personal Health Records

in Cloud Computing Environments–An Experimental Exploration of the Impact of Storage

Solutions and Data Breaches. 1-15.

Adorjan, M., & Ricciardelli, R. (2019). A New Privacy Paradox? Youth Agentic Practices of Privacy

Management Despite "Nothing to Hide" Online. *Canadian Review of Sociology/Revue*

canadienne de sociologie, 56(1), 8-29.

Ajumobi, O. D. (2014). *Alignment of human competencies with mobile technology and business*

strategy in women-led SMEs (Doctoral book, University of Cape Town). 1-137.

Aleisa, N., & Renaud, K. (2017a). Privacy of the Internet of Things: A Systematic Literature Review. In *Proceedings of the 50th Hawaii International Conference on System Sciences*. 5947-

5956.

Aleisa, N., & Renaud, K. (2017b). Yes, I know this IoT Device Might Invade my Privacy, but I Love

it Anyway! A Study of Saudi Arabian Perceptions. *In Proceedings of the 2nd International*

Conference on Internet of Things, Big Data and Security. 109-205.

Alexandrou, A., & Chen, L. C. (2016). A security risk perception model for the adoption of mobile

devices in the healthcare industry. *Security Journal*, 1-25.

Aljallad, Z. (2019). Designing a Mobile Application to Support Social Processes for Privacy. In *The*

2019 NDSS Workshop on Usable Security and Privacy. 1-12.

Alladi, T., Chamola, V., Sikdar, B., & Choo, K. K. R. (2020). Consumer IoT: Security vulnerability

case studies and solutions. *IEEE Consumer Electronics Magazine, 9*(2), 17-25.

Anand, S. S., & Mobasher, B. (2003). Intelligent techniques for web personalization. Proceedings of the 2003 international conference on intelligent techniques for web personalization (pp. 1–36). Berlin: Springer-Verlag.

Arif, I., Afshan, S., & Sharif, A. (2016). Resistance to mobile banking adoption in a developing country: Evidence from modified TAM. *Journal of Finance and Economics Research*, *1*(1), 25-42.

Attié, E., & Meyer-Waarden, L. (2018). The Acceptance Process of the Internet of Things, 21-46. In the Book "Smart Marketing With the Internet of Things". Editors Simoes, D, Barbosa, B & Filipe, S. IGI Global, Hershey, PA.

Babar, S., Stango, A., Prasad, N., Sen, J., & Prasad, R. (2011). Proposed embedded security framework for internet of things (iot). In *Wireless Communication, Vehicular Technology, Information Theory and Aerospace & Electronic Systems Technology (Wireless VITAE), 2011 2nd International Conference on* (pp. 1-5). IEEE.

Babbie, E. R. (2015). *The Practice of Social Research*. Cengage Learning. Retrieved from: https://books.google.co.za/books?hl=en&lr=&id=bS9BBAAAQBAJ&oi=fnd&pg=PR5&ots=Pwp27RqpR1&sig=bqSSruFhhtrM-Sjr_1UECbBlibY#v=onepage&q&f=false

Baek, Y. M. (2014). Solving the privacy paradox: A counter-argument experimental approach. *Computers in Human Behavior*, *38*, 33-42.

Barth, S., de Jong, M. D., Junger, M., Hartel, P. H., & Roppelt, J. C. (2019). Putting the privacy paradox to the test: Online privacy and security behaviors among users with technical knowledge, privacy awareness, and financial resources. *Telematics and Informatics*.

Bauer, C., Schmid, K. S., & Strauss, C. (2018). An Open Model for Researching the Role of Culture in Online Self-Disclosure. In *Proceedings of the 51st Hawaii International Conference on System Sciences*. 3637-3646.

Beiske, B. (2002). Research methods. Uses and limitations of questionnaires, interviews, and case studies. GRIN Verlag.

Belanger, F., & Crossler, R. E. (2019). Dealing with digital traces: Understanding protective behaviors on mobile devices. *The Journal of Strategic Information Systems*, *28*(1), 34-49.

Belanger, F., & Xu, H. (2015). The role of information systems research in shaping the future of information privacy. *Information Systems Journal*, *25*(6), 573-578.

Beldad, A. D., & Hegner, S. M. (2017). More Photos From Me to Thee: Factors Influencing the Intention to Continue Sharing Personal Photos on an Online Social Networking (OSN) Site among Young Adults in the Netherlands. *International Journal of Human–Computer Interaction*, *33*(5), 410-422.

Bertino, E., & Islam, N. (2017). Botnets and Internet of Things Security. *Computer*, *50*(2), 76-79.

Beuker, S. (2016). *Privacy paradox: Factors influencing disclosure of personal information among*

German and Dutch SNS users (Master's book, University of Twente). 1-93.

Beyer, C. (2014). Mobile Security: A Literature Review. *International Journal of Computer Applications, 97(8)*, 9-11.

Bhattacherjee, A. (2012). *Social Science Research: Principles, methods, and practices*. Global Text Project. Retrieved from Open Access Textbooks. http://scholarcommons.usf.edu/cgi/viewcontent.cgi?article=1002&context=oa_textbooks

Blank, G., Bolsover, G., & Dubois, E. (2014). A new privacy paradox: Young people and privacy on social network sites. *Prepared for the Annual Meeting of the American Sociological Association*. 1-33.

Blythe, J. M., & Johnson, S. D. (2018). The consumer security index for IoT: A protocol for developing an index to improve consumer decision making and to incentivize greater security provision in IoT devices. In *Living in the Internet of Things: Cybersecurity of the IoT-2018*, IET.1-7.

Boehmer, J., LaRose, R., Rifon, N., Alhabash, S., & Cotten, S. (2015). Determinants of online safety behaviour: towards an intervention strategy for college students. *Behaviour & Information Technology*, *34*(10), 1022-1035.

Bolarinwa, O. A. (2015). Principles and methods of validity and reliability testing of questionnaires used in social and health science researches. *Nigerian Postgraduate Medical Journal*, *22*(4), 195-201.

Botha, J., Grobler, M. M., Hahn, J., & Eloff, M. (2017). A High-Level Comparison Between the South African Protection of Personal Information Act and International Data Protection Laws. In *ICMLG2017 5th International Conference on Management Leadership and Governance* (p. 57-68). Academic Conferences and publishing limited.

Brinson, N., & Rutherford, D. (2016). Quantified Self and Personal Health Privacy Policy Limitations. 1-27.

Brown, B. (2001). Studying the Internet experience. *HP LABORATORIES TECHNICAL REPORT HPL*, 1-23.

Bryman, A., & Bell, E. (2015). *Business research methods*. Oxford University Press, USA. Retrieved from:https://books.google.co.za/books?hl=en&lr=&id=l7u6BwAAQBAJ&oi=fnd&pg=PP1&dq=Bryman,+A.+%26+Bell,+E.+(2011).+Business+Research+Methods.+3rd+edition.+New+York:+Oxford+University+Press.+&ots=AvTkw8LWLo&sig=zmF06DuRIImw7C9-Ecq0-P-Kjog#v=onepage&q&f=false

Buchanan, T., Paine, C., Joinson, A. N., & Reips, U. D. (2007). Development of measures of online privacy concern and protection for use on the Internet. *Journal of the American society for information science and technology*, *58*(2), 157-165.

Buchwald, A., Letner, A., Urbach, N., & von Entreß-Fürsteneck, M. (2017). Towards Explaining the Willingness to Disclose Personal Self-Tracking Data To Service Providers. 3071-3081.

BusinessTech. (2019). Mimecast research finds impersonation, phishing attacks on the rise in South Africa. Retrieved November, 09, 2019. From: https://businesstech.co.za/news/industry-news/320058/mimecast-research-finds-impersonation-phishing-attacks-on-the-rise-in-south-africa/

Byrne, B. M. Routledge; New York: 2013. *Structural Equation Modelling With AMOS: Basic Concepts, Applications, and Programming.* 1-438.

Cangur, S., & Ercan, I. (2015). Comparison of Model Fit Indices Used in Structural Equation Modeling Under Multivariate Normality. *Journal of Modern Applied Statistical Methods.* 14(1), 152-167.

Cao, T. D., Hoang, H. H., Huynh, H. X., Nguyen, B. M., Pham, T. V., Tran-Minh, Q., & Truong, H. L. (2016). Iot services for solving critical problems in vietnam: A research landscape and directions. *IEEE Internet Computing, 20*(5), 76-81.

Carignani, A., & Gemmo, V. (2018). New Media and Privacy the Privacy Paradox in the Digital World: I Will Not Disclose My Data. Actually, I Will... It Depends. *International Journal of Computer (IJC), 27*(1), 201-212.

Caron, X., Bosua, R., Maynard, S. B., & Ahmad, A. (2016). The Internet of Things (IoT) and its impact on individual privacy: An Australian perspective. *Computer Law & Security Review, 32*(1), 4-15.

Castro, P., & Bettencourt, L. (2017). Exploring the predictors and the role of trust and concern in the context of data disclosure to governmental institutions. *Behaviour & Information Technology, 36*(3), 321-331.

Cavana, R., Delahaye, B., & Sekeran, U. (2001). *Applied business research: Qualitative and quantitative methods.* John Wiley & Sons.

Chang, S. E., Liu, A. Y., & Shen, W. C. (2017). User trust in social networking services: A comparison of Facebook and LinkedIn. *Computers in Human Behavior, 69*, 207-217.

Chellappa, R. K., Sin, G. H. R., & Jia, J. (2014). Competing for Information: A Duopoly of Personalized Service Provision under Privacy Concerns. *Theory in Economics of Information Systems.* 1-51.

Chen, D., Bovornkeeratiroj, P., Irwin, D., & Shenoy, P. (2018, July). Private Memoirs of IoT Devices: Safeguarding User Privacy in the IoT Era. In *Proceedings of the 38th IEEE International Conference on Distributed Computing Systems (ICDCS'18).* 1-10.

Chen, H. T., & Chen, W. (2015). Couldn't or wouldn't? The influence of privacy concerns and self-efficacy in privacy management on privacy protection. *Cyberpsychology, Behavior, and Social Networking, 18*(1), 13-19.

Chen, R., & Sharma, S. K. (2015). Learning and self-disclosure behavior on social networking sites: the case of Facebook users. *European Journal of Information Systems, 24*(1), 93-106.

Cheung, C., Lee, Z. W., & Chan, T. K. (2015). Self-disclosure in social networking sites: the role of perceived cost, perceived benefits and social influence. *Internet Research, 25*(2), 279-299.

Choi, H., Park, J., & Jung, Y. (2018). The role of privacy fatigue in online privacy behavior. *Computers in Human Behavior, 81*, 42-51.

Choi, J., & Kim, S. (2016). Is the smartwatch an IT product or a fashion product? A study on factors affecting the intention to use smartwatches. *Computers in Human Behavior, 63*, 777-786.

Choudhury, R. R., Basak, S., & Guha, D. (2013). Cyber crimes - Challenges & Solutions. *International Journal of Computer Science and Information Technologies, 4*(5), 729-732.

Church, A. H., & Waclawski, J. (2001). *Designing and using organizational surveys: A seven-step process.* John Wiley & Sons. Retrieved from: https://books.google.co.za/books?hl=en&lr=&id=gD6zDwAAQBAJ&oi=fnd&pg=PR21&ots=ihd5V5KeHh&sig=mLirHr079fYSFSwrpTyviTAM-iE&redir_esc=y#v=onepage&q&f=false

Conti, M., Dehghantanha, A., Franke, K., & Watson, S. (2018). Internet of Things security and forensics: Challenges and opportunities. 1-7.

Correia, J., & Compeau, D. (2017, January). Information Privacy Awareness (IPA): A Review of the Use, Definition and Measurement of IPA. In *Proceedings of the 50th Hawaii International Conference on System Sciences*. 4021-4030.

Creswell, J. W. (2013). *Research Design Qualitative, Quantitative, and Mixed Methods Approaches.* (V. Knight, K. Koscielak, B. Bauhaus, M. Markanish, & A. Hutchinson, Eds.) (4th ed.). California: Sage Publications. Retrieved from: https://books.google.co.za/books?hl=en&lr=&id=EbogAQAAQBAJ&oi=fnd&pg=PR1&dq=Research+Design+Qualitative,+Quantitative,+and+Mixed+Methods+Approaches&ots=cacRtRTuB4&sig=VLTLAYwQUSoBHV-fcayGZ5P38C0#v=onepage&q=Research%20Design%20Qualitative%2C%20Quantitative%2C%20and%20M&f=false

Creswell, J. W., & Clark, V. L. P. (2007). *Designing and conducting mixed methods research.* London, UK: Sage Publications.

Crossler, R. E., & Bélanger, F. (2017, January). The Mobile Privacy-Security Knowledge Gap Model: Understanding Behaviors. In *Proceedings of the 50th Hawaii International Conference on System Sciences*. 4071-4080.

Crossler, R., & Bélanger, F. (2014). An extended perspective on individual security behaviors: Protection motivation theory and a unified security practices (USP) instrument. *ACM SIGMIS Database, 45*(4), 51-71.

Crotty, M. (1998). *The foundations of social research: Meaning and perspective in the research process.* Sage. Retrieved From: https://books.google.co.za/books?hl=en&lr=&id=yV-JCwAAQBAJ&oi=fnd&pg=PR5&ots=PZ_q002Wa6&sig=gCGhw6tUf0NVyybTdjqVXcBLOlQ&redir_esc=y#v=onepage&q&f=false

Da Xu, L., He, W., & Li, S. (2014). Internet of things in industries: A survey. *IEEE Transactions on industrial informatics, 10*(4), 2233-2243.

Das, S., Kramer, A. D., Dabbish, L. A., & Hong, J. I. (2014, November). Increasing security sensitivity with social proof: A large-scale experimental confirmation. In *Proceedings of the 2014 ACM SIGSAC conference on computer and communications security* (pp. 739-749).

Demo, G., Neiva, E. R., Nunes, I., & Rozzett, K. (2012). Human resources management policies and practices scale (HRMPPS): Exploratory and confirmatory factor analysis. *BAR-Brazilian Administration Review, 9*(4), 395-420.

Dienlin, T., & Metzger, M. J. (2016). An Extended Privacy Calculus Model for SNSs: Analyzing Self-Disclosure and Self-Withdrawal in a Representative US Sample. *Journal of Computer-Mediated Communication, 21*(5), 368-383.

Dikow, H., Hasan, O., Kosch, H., Brunie, L., & Sornin, R. (2015). Improving the Accuracy of Business-to-Business (B2B) Reputation Systems Through Rater Expertise Prediction. *Computing, 97*(1), 29-49.

Dincelli, E., & Zhou, X. (2017). Examining self-disclosure on wearable devices: The roles of benefit structure and privacy calculus. *Proceedings of 23rd Americas Conference on Information Systems 2017*, 1-5.

Dinev, T., & Hart, P. (2006). An extended privacy calculus model for e-commerce transactions. *Information Systems Research, 17*(1), 61-80.

Doig, J. M. (2016). *Impact of online privacy concerns and brand reputation on consumer willingness to provide personal information* (Doctoral book, Queensland University of Technology). Retrieved from: https://eprints.qut.edu.au/91648/1/Jennifer_Doig_book.pdf

Dong, X., Clark, J., & Jacob, J. (2010). Defending the weakest link: phishing websites detection by analysing user behaviours. *Telecommunication Systems, 45*, 215-226.

Farooq, M. U., Waseem, M., Khairi, A., & Mazhar, S. (2015). A critical analysis on the security concerns of internet of things (IoT). *International Journal of Computer Applications, 111*(7), 1-6.

Fornell, C., & Larcker, D. F. (1981). Evaluating structural equation models with unobservable variables and measurement error. *Marketing Research Journal*, 18(1), 39-50.

Fremantle, P., Aziz, B., & Kirkham, T. (2017, March). Enhancing IoT Security and privacy with distributed ledgers-a position paper. In *IoTBDS 2017: 2nd Interantional Conference on Internet of Things, Big Data and Security*. SCITEPRESS–Science and Technology Publications.

Furfaro, A., Argento, L., Parise, A., & Piccolo, A. (2017). Using virtual environments for the assessment of cybersecurity issues in IoT scenarios. *Simulation Modelling Practice and Theory, 73*, 43-54.

Gabriele, S., & Chiasson, S. (2020, April). Understanding Fitness Tracker Users' Security and Privacy Knowledge, Attitudes and Behaviours. In *Proceedings of the 2020 CHI Conference on Human Factors in Computing Systems* (pp. 1-12).

Gan, G., Lu, Z., & Jiang, J. (2011, August). Internet of things security analysis. In *Internet Technology and Applications (iTAP), 2011 International Conference on* (pp. 1-4). IEEE.

Garrido, M., Sey, A., Hart, T. B., & Santana, L. (2012). Exploratory study on explanations and theories of how Telecentres and other community-based e-Inclusion actors operate and have an impact on digital and social inclusion policy goals. *Institute for Prospective Technological Studies*, 1-154.

Glasow, P. (2005). *Fundamentals of Survey Research Methodology.* Washington: Washington C3 Center. 1-11.

Gómez-Barroso, J. L., Feijóo, C., & Martínez-Martínez, I. J. (2018). Privacy calculus: Factors that influence the perception of benefit. *El profesional de la información (EPI)*, *27*(2), 341-348.

Gray, D. (2013). *Doing Research in the Real World*. (A. Jarold, R. Lupton, I. Anticliff, & C. Bitten, Eds.) (3rd ed.). London: Sage Publications. Retrieved from: https://books.google.co.za/books?hl=en&lr=&id=N_WGAwAAQBAJ&oi=fnd&pg=PP1&dq=exploratory++research+purpose&ots=QtTQh-36wl&sig=HCCj_hcziNji8A7euoizXXqgcj8#v=onepage&q=timeframe&f=false

Green, J. L., Camilli, G., & Elmore, P. B. (2012). *Handbook of complementary methods in education research. Foundations* (Revise). Lawrence Erlbaum Associates. Retrieved from: http://www.google.com/books?id=pt2JBMMlQG0C

Gross, R., & Acquisti, A. (2005). Information revelation and privacy in online social networks. In *Proceedings of the 2005 ACM workshop on Privacy in the electronic society* (pp. 71-80). ACM.

Hair Jr, J., Sarstedt, M., Hopkins, L., & G. Kuppelwieser, V. (2014). Partial least squares structural equation modeling (PLS-SEM) An emerging tool in business research. *European Business Review, 26*(2), 106-121

Hair, J. F., Black, W. C., Babin, B. J., Anderson, R. E., & Tatham, R. L. (2006). Multivariate data analysis 6th Edition. *Pearson Prentice Hall. New Jersey. humans: Critique and reformulation. Journal of Abnormal Psychology, 87*, 49-74.

Hair, J. F., Ringle, C. M., & Sarstedt, M. (2014). PLS-SEM: Indeed a silver bullet. *Journal of Marketing theory and Practice, 19*(2), 139-152.

Hair, J.F., Hult, G.T.M., Ringle, C.M. and Sarstedt, M. (2017). A Primer on Partial Least Squares Structural Equation Modeling (PLS-SEM). *Sage, Thousand Oaks.*

Hajli, N., & Lin, X. (2016). Exploring the security of information sharing on social networking sites: The role of perceived control of information. *Journal of Business Ethics, 133*(1), 111-123.

Hallam, C., & Zanella, G. (2016). Wearable device data and privacy: A study of perception and behavior. *World, 7*(1), 82-91.

Hallam, C., & Zanella, G. (2017). Online self-disclosure: The privacy paradox explained as a temporally discounted balance between concerns and rewards. *Computers in Human Behavior, 68*, 217-227.

Han, M., Shen, S., Zhou, Y., Xu, Z., Miao, T., & Qi, J. (2019). An Analysis of the Cause of Privacy Paradox among SNS Users: take Chinese College Students as an Example. In *Proceedings of the 52nd Hawaii International Conference on System Sciences*. 1615 – 1624.

Hargittai, E., & Marwick, A. (2016). "What can I really do?" Explaining the privacy paradox with online apathy. *International Journal of Communication, 10*, 1-21.

Hedayati, A. (2012). An analysis of identity theft: Motives, related frauds, techniques and prevention. *Journal of Law and Conflict Resolution, 4*, 1-12.

Hein, D. W., Jodoin, J. L., Rauschnabel, P. A., & Ivens, B. S. (2018). Are wearables good or bad for society?: An exploration of societal benefits, risks, and consequences of augmented reality smart glasses. In *Wearable Technologies: Concepts, Methodologies, Tools, and Applications* (pp. 1313-1337). IGI Global.

Hellerstein, J. M. (2008). Quantitative data cleaning for large databases. *United Nations Economic Commission for Europe (UNECE)*. 1-42.

Henseler, J., Ringle, C. M., & Sarstedt, M. (2014). A new criterion for assessing discriminant validity in variance-based structural equation modeling. *Journal of the Academy of Marketing Science*. 43(1), 115–135.

Henze, M., Hermerschmidt, L., Kerpen, D., Häußling, R., Rumpe, B., & Wehrle, K. (2016). A comprehensive approach to privacy in the cloud-based Internet of Things. *Future Generation Computer Systems*, *56*, 701-718.

Hossain, M. M., & Prybutok, V. R. (2008). Consumer acceptance of RFID technology: An exploratory study. *IEEE transactions on engineering management*, *55*(2), 316-328.

Hsu, C. L., & Lin, J. C. C. (2016). An empirical examination of consumer adoption of Internet of Things services: Network externalities and concern for information privacy perspectives. Computers in Human Behavior, 62, 516-527.

Huang, C. C., Wang, Y. M., Wu, T. W., & Wang, P. A. (2013). An empirical analysis of the antecedents and performance consequences of using the moodle platform. *International Journal of Information and Education Technology*, *3*(2), 217-221.

Hunt, D. S., Lin, C. A., & Atkin, D. J. (2014). Photo-messaging: Adopter attributes, technology factors and use motives. *Computers in Human Behavior*, *40*, 171-179.

Ifinedo, P. (2012). Understanding information systems security policy compliance: An integration of the theory of planned behaviour and the protection motivation theory. *Computers & Security*, *31*(1), 83-95.

Iqbal, M. A., Olaleye, O. G., & Bayoumi, M. A. (2017). A Review on Internet of Things (IoT): Security and Privacy Requirements and the Solution Approaches. *Global Journal of Computer Science and Technology, 16*(7), 1-9.

Irshad, M. (2016). A Systematic Review of Information Security Frameworks in the Internet of Things (IoT). In *High Performance Computing and Communications; IEEE 14th International Conference on Smart City; IEEE 2nd International Conference on Data Science and Systems (HPCC/SmartCity/DSS), 2016 IEEE 18th International Conference on* (pp. 1270-1275).

Jerkins, J. A. (2017). Motivating a market or regulatory solution to IoT insecurity with the Mirai botnet code. In *Computing and Communication Workshop and Conference (CCWC), 2017 IEEE 7th Annual* (pp. 1-5).

Jiang, Z., Heng, C. S., & Choi, B. C. (2013). Research note—privacy concerns and privacy-protective behavior in synchronous online social interactions. *Information Systems Research, 24*(3), 579-595.

Kehr, F., Wentzel, D., Kowatsch, T., & Fleisch, E. (2015). Rethinking Privacy Decisions: Pre-Existing Attitudes, Pre-Existing Emotional States, and a Situational Privacy Calculus. Association for Information Systems. *Twenty-Third European Conference on Information Systems (ECIS),* 1-15.

Keith, M. J., Thompson, S. C., Hale, J., Lowry, P. B., & Greer, C. (2013). Information disclosure on mobile devices: Re-examining privacy calculus with actual user behavior. *International Journal of Human-Computer Studies, 71*(12), 1163-1173.

Kietzmann, J., Pitt, L., McCarthy, I., & Schau, H. (2018). Introduction to the Minitrack on Wearable Technology and the Internet of Everything. In *Proceedings of the 51st Hawaii International Conference on System Sciences, 3995-3996.*

Killam, L. (2013). *Research terminology simplified: Paradigms, axiology, ontology, epistemology and methodology.* Retireved from: https://books.google.co.za/books?hl=en&lr=&id=nKMnAgAAQBAJ&oi=fnd&pg=PA3&dq=Paradigms,+Axiology,+Ontology,+Epistemology+and+Methodology&ots=u4N8tQanIK&sig=14q5X5XRs1ikNkwz-K-mJuxAUwI&redir_esc=y#v=onepage&q=Paradigms%2C%20Axiology%2C%20Ontology%2C%20Epistemology%20and%20Methodology&f=false

Kim, D., Park, K., Park, Y., & Ahn, J. H. (2019). Willingness to provide personal information: Perspective of privacy calculus in IoT services. *Computers in Human Behavior, 92*, 273-281.

Kim, M. S., & Kim, S. (2018). Factors influencing willingness to provide personal information for personalized recommendations. *Computers in Human Behavior, 88*, 143-152.

Kisekka, V., Bagchi-Sen, S., & Rao, H. R. (2013). Extent of private information disclosure on online social networks: An exploration of Facebook mobile phone users. *Computers in human behavior, 29*(6), 2722-2729.

Klein, H. K., & Myers, M. D. (1999). A set of principles for conducting and evaluating interpretive field studies in information systems. *MIS quarterly*, 67-93.

Knowles, B., Beck, S., Finney, J., Devine, J., & Lindley, J. (2019). A Scenario-Based Methodology for Exploring Risks: Children and Programmable IoT. In *Proceedings of the 2019 on Designing Interactive Systems Conference* (pp. 751-761).

Kokolakis, S. (2017). Privacy attitudes and privacy behaviour: A review of current research on the privacy paradox phenomenon. *Computers & Security, 64*, 122-134.

Koskinen, K. U., Pihlanto, P., & Vanharanta, H. (2003). Tacit knowledge acquisition and sharing in a project work context. *International journal of project management, 21*(4), 281-290.

Kowatsch, T., & Maass, W. (2012). Critical privacy factors of internet of things services: an empirical investigation with domain experts. In *Knowledge and Technologies in Innovative Information Systems* (pp. 200-211). Springer, Berlin, Heidelberg.

Krasnova, H., Kolesnikova, E., & Guenther, O. (2009). " It won't happen to me!": self-disclosure in online social networks. *Proceedings of the Fifteenth Americas Conference on Information Systems, 1-9.*

Krasnova, H., Spiekermann, S., Koroleva, K., & Hildebrand, T. (2010). Online social networks: Why we disclose. *Journal of information technology, 25*(2), 109-125.

Krasnova, H., Veltri, N. F., & Günther, O. (2012). Self-disclosure and privacy calculus on social networking sites: The role of culture. *Business & Information Systems Engineering, 4*(3), 127-135.

Kritzinger, E. (2017). Cultivating a cyber-safety culture among school learners in South Africa. *Africa Education Review*, 1-20.

Kumar, V. (2012). Prevent/Control Identity Theft: Impact on Trust and Consumers' Purchase Intention in B2C EC. *Information Resources Management Journal, 25*, 30-60.

Lai, C. Y., Liang, T. P., & Hui, K. L. (2018). Information privacy paradox: A neural science study. *Information Privacy, 6*, 26-2018.

Lawson, S. T., Yeo, S. K., Yu, H., & Greene, E. (2016). The cyber-doom effect: The impact of fear appeals in the US cyber security debate. In *Cyber Conflict (CyCon), 2016 8th International Conference on* (pp. 65-80).

Lee-Won, R. J., Shim, M., Joo, Y. K., & Park, S. G. (2014). Who puts the best "face" forward on Facebook?: Positive self-presentation in online social networking and the role of self-consciousness, actual-to-total Friends ratio, and culture. *Computers in Human Behavior, 39*, 413-423.

Lee, H., Park, H., & Kim, J. (2013). Why do people share their context information on Social Network Services? A qualitative study and an experimental study on users' behavior of balancing perceived benefit and risk. *International Journal of Human-Computer Studies, 71*(9), 862-877.

Lee, I., & Lee, K. (2015). The Internet of Things (IoT): Applications, investments, and challenges for enterprises. *Business Horizons, 58*(4), 431-440.

Lee, L., Lee, J., Egelman, S., & Wagner, D. (2016). Information disclosure concerns in the age of wearable computing. In *NDSS Workshop on Usable Security (USEC)* (Vol. 1). 1-10.

Lee, S. K., Bae, M., & Kim, H. (2017). Future of IoT Networks: A Survey. *Applied Sciences, 7*(10), 1072-1096.

Lee, Y., & Larsen, K. R. (2009). Threat or coping appraisal: determinants of SMB executives' decision to adopt anti-malware software. *European Journal of Information Systems, 18*(2), 177-187.

Li, D. C. (2011). Online social network acceptance: a social perspective. *Internet Research, 21*(5), 562-580.

Li, S., Da Xu, L., & Zhao, S. (2018). 5G internet of things: A survey. *Journal of Industrial Information Integration.* 1-9.

Llbaque-Saenz, C. F., Chang, Y., Kim, J., Park, M. C., & Rho, J. J. (2016). The role of perceived information practices on consumers' intention to authorise secondary use of personal data. *Behaviour & Information Technology, 35*(5), 339-356.

Lindberg, D. (2011). Prevention of Identity theft : A Review of the Literature. *Criminology and Criminal Justice, 10*, 1-11.

Liu, Z., Min, Q., Zhai, Q., & Smyth, R. (2016). Self-disclosure in Chinese micro-blogging: A social exchange theory perspective. *Information & Management, 53*(1), 53-63.

Llamas, R., Ubrani, J., & Shirer, M. (2019). Worldwide Wearables Shipments Surge 94.6% in 3Q 2019 Led by Expanding Hearables Market. Retrieved From: https://www.idc.com/getdoc.jsp?containerId=prUS45712619

Lopez, J., Rios, R., Bao, F., & Wang, G. (2017). Evolving privacy: From sensors to the Internet of Things. *Future Generation Computer Systems*, *75*, 46-57.

Lourie, G. (2017, August 22). Why Cape Town is One of the World's Smart Cities?. *Talk IoT*. Retreived from https://talkiot.co.za/2017/08/22/cape-town-one-worlds-smart-cities/

Macada, A., & Luciano, E. (2010). The influence of human factors on vulnerability to information security breaches. *Proceedings of the Sixteenth Americas Conference on Information Systems* (pp. 1-9). Lima: Americas Conference on Information Systems.

Macha, W., & Kadakia, A. (2017). Education in South Africa. Retrieved from: https://wenr.wes.org/2017/05/education-south-africa

Markantonakis, K. (2017, August). An exploratory analysis of the security risks of the Internet of Things in finance. In *International Conference on Trust and Privacy in Digital Business* (pp. 164-179). Springer, Cham.

Matt, C., Becker, M., Kolbeck, A., & Hess, T. (2019). Continuously Healthy, Continuously Used?–A Thematic Analysis of User Perceptions on Consumer Health Wearables. *Pacific Asia Journal of the Association for Information Systems*, *11*(1). 108 – 132.

Mendel, T., & Toch, E. (2017). Susceptibility to Social Influence of Privacy Behaviors: Peer versus Authoritative Sources. In *Proceedings of the 2017 ACM Conference on Computer Supported Cooperative Work and Social Computing* (pp. 581-593).

Min, J., & Kim, B. (2015). How are people enticed to disclose personal information despite privacy concerns in social network sites? The calculus between benefit and cost. *Journal of the Association for Information Science and Technology*, *66*(4), 839-857.

Mingers, J. (2001). Combining IS research methods: towards a pluralist methodology. *Information systems research*, *12*(3), 240-259.

Mohamed, N., & Ahmad, I. H. (2012). Information privacy concerns, antecedents and privacy measure use in social networking sites: Evidence from Malaysia. *Computers in Human Behavior*, *28*(6), 2366-2375.

Morando, F., Iemma, R., & Raiteri, E. (2014). Privacy evaluation: what empirical research on users' valuation of personal data tells us. *Internet Policy Review*, *3*(2), 1-11.

Myers, M. (2009). *Qualitative research in business and management*. London: Sage Publications.

Myers, M. D. (2013). *Qualitative research in business and management*. London, UK: Sage Publications. Retrieved From: https://books.google.co.za/books?hl=en&lr=&id=XZARAgAAQBAJ&oi=fnd&pg=PP2&dq=Myers,+M.+D.+(2013).+Qualitative+research+in+business+and+management.+London,+UK:+Sage+Publications.&ots=CaKHpn4a3b&sig=S0ozzj16uNZD3XrJQRaApxYT2mI#v=onepage&q&f=false

Myerscough, S., Lowe, B., & Alpert, F. (2008). Willingness to provide personal information online: The role of perceived privacy risk, privacy statements and brand strength. *Journal of Website Promotion*, *2*(1-2), 115-140.

Mzekandaba, S. (2016, February 29). *ITWeb*. Retrieved from ITWeb: http://www.itweb.co.za/index.php?option=com_content&view=article&id=150229

Naeini, P. E., Bhagavatula, S., Habib, H., Degeling, M., Bauer, L., Cranor, L., & Sadeh, N. (2017, July). Privacy Expectations and Preferences in an IoT World. In *Symposium on Usable Privacy and Security (SOUPS)*. 399-412.

Neumann, W. L. (1994). Social research methods: Qualitative and quantitative approaches. 2d ed. Needham Heights, MA: Allyn & Bacon.

Ng, M. (2014). Consumer motivations to disclose information and participate in commercial activities on Facebook. *Journal of Global Scholars of Marketing Science*, *24*(4), 365-383.

Niemietz, M., Somorovsky, J., Mainka, C., & Schwenk, J. (2015). Not so smart: On smart TV apps. In *Secure Internet of Things (SIoT), 2015 International Workshop on* (pp. 72-81). IEEE.

Norberg, P. A., Horne, D. R., & Horne, D. A. (2007). The privacy paradox: Personal information disclosure intentions versus behaviors. *Journal of Consumer Affairs*, *41*(1), 100-126.

Novotny, Á., Dávid, L., & Csáfor, H. (2015). Applying RFID technology in the retail industry-benefits and concerns from the consumer's perspective. *Amfiteatru Economic*, *17*(39), 615-631.

Orlikowski, W. J., & Baroudi, J. J. (1991). Studying information technology in organizations: Research approaches and assumptions. *Information systems research*, *2*(1), 1-28.

Ortiz, J., Chih, W. H., & Tsai, F. S. (2018). Information privacy, consumer alienation, and lurking behavior in social networking sites. *Computers in Human Behavior*, *80*, 143-157.

Peng, S., Yang, A., Cao, L., Yu, S., & Xie, D. (2017). Social influence modeling using information theory in mobile social networks. *Information Sciences*, *379*, 146-159.

Ponciano, L., Barbosa, P., Brasileiro, F., Brito, A., & Andrade, N. (2017). Designing for Pragmatists and Fundamentalists: Privacy Concerns and Attitudes on the Internet of Things. In *Proceedings of the XVI Brazilian Symposium on Human Factors in Computing Systems* (p. 21-30). ACM.

Preibusch, S., Krol, K., & Beresford, A. R. (2013). The privacy economics of voluntary over-disclosure in Web forms. In *The Economics of Information Security and Privacy* (pp. 183-209). Springer, Berlin, Heidelberg.

Prince, C. (2018). Do consumers want to control their personal data? Empirical evidence. *International Journal of Human-Computer Studies*, *110*, 21-32.

Pu, Y., & Grossklags, J. (2016). Towards a model on the factors influencing social app users' valuation of interdependent privacy. *Proceedings on Privacy Enhancing Technologies, 2016*(2), 61-81.

PwC, H. (2014). Health wearables: Early days. *Pricewaterhousecoopers, Top Health Industry Issues. Wearable Devices*. Retrieved from: https://www.pwc.com/us/en/health-industries/top-health-industry-issues/assets/pwc-hri-wearable-devices.pdf

Qualtrics (2019). Sample Size Calculator. Retrieved From: https://www.qualtrics.com/blog/calculating-sample-size/

Ranzini, G., Etter, M., & Vermeulen, I. E. (2017). Privacy in the sharing economy: European Perspectives. *Report from the EU H2020 Research Project Ps2Share: Participation, Privacy, and Power in the Sharing Economy*, 1-18.

Roky, H., & Meriouh, Y. Al. (2015). Evaluation by Users of an Industrial Information System (XPPS) Based on the DeLone and McLean Model for IS Success. *Procedia Economics and Finance*. 26, 903-913.

Román-Castro, R., López, J., & Gritzalis, S. (2018). Evolution and trends in IoT security. *Computer, 51*(7), 16-25.

Roman, R., Zhou, J., & Lopez, J. (2013). On the features and challenges of security and privacy in distributed internet of things. *Computer Networks, 57*(10), 2266-2279.

Rönkkö, M., McIntosh, C. N., Antonakis, J., & Edwards, J. R. (2016). Partial least squares path modeling: Time for some serious second thoughts. *Journal of Operations Management, 47*, 9-27.

Rui, J., & Stefanone, M. A. (2013). Strategic self-presentation online: A cross-cultural study. *Computers in Human Behavior, 29*(1), 110-118.

Saeri, A. K., Ogilvie, C., La Macchia, S. T., Smith, J. R., & Louis, W. R. (2014). Predicting Facebook users' online privacy protection: Risk, trust, norm focus theory, and the theory of planned behavior. *The Journal of social psychology*, *154*(4), 352-369.

Safiih, M., & Azreen, N. (2016). Confirmatory Factor Analysis Approach: A Case Study of Mathematics Students' Achievement in TIMSS. *Malaysian Journal of Mathematical Sciences*, *10*, 41-51.

Salahuddin, M., & Gow, J. (2016). The effects of internet usage, financial development and trade openness on economic growth in South Africa: A time series analysis. Telematics and Informatics, 33(4), 1141-1154.

Sanchez, G. (2013). PLS path modeling with R. *Berkeley: Trowchez Editions*, *383-605*.

Sartain, JD. (2015). Top security tools in the fight against cybercrime. [Web log post]. Retrieved from: http://www.networkworld.com/article/2922730/security0/top-security-tools-in-the-fight-against-cybercrime.html

Saunders, M., Lewis, P., & Thornhill, A. (2009). Research methods for business students fifth edition (5th ed.). England: Pearson Education Limited.

Saunders, M., Lewis, P., & Thornhill, A. (2015). Research methods for business students fifth edition (5th ed.). England: Pearson Education Limited.

Schaefer, D. R., & Dillman, D. A. (1998). Development of a standard e-mail methodology: Results of an experiment. *Public opinion quarterly*, 62(3), 378-397.

Scharnick, N., Gerber, M., & Futcher, L. (2016). Review of data storage protection approaches for POPI compliance. In *Information Security for South Africa (ISSA), 2016* (pp. 48-55).

Schomakers, E. M., Lidynia, C., Müllmann, D., & Ziefle, M. (2019). Internet users' perceptions of information sensitivity–insights from germany. *International Journal of Information Management*, *46*, 142-150.

Sharma, S., & Crossler, R. E. (2014). Disclosing too much? Situational factors affecting information disclosure in social commerce environment. *Electronic Commerce Research and Applications, 13*(5), 305-319.

Shibchurn, J., & Van, X. B. (2014). Investigating effects of monetary reward on information disclosure by online social networks users. In *System Sciences (HICSS), 2014 47th Hawaii International Conference on* (pp. 1725-1734).

Shyu, C., Li, Y., & Tang, Y. (2013). Applying Confirmatory Factor Analysis on the Measure for Restaurant Over-service. *The Journal of International Management Studies, 8*, 10-16.

Sicari, S., Rizzardi, A., Grieco, L. A., & Coen-Porisini, A. (2015). Security, privacy and trust in Internet of Things: The road ahead. *Computer Networks, 76*, 146-164.

Sillaber, C., & Breu, R. (2015). Using Business Process Model Awareness to improve Stakeholder Participation in Information Systems Security Risk Management Processes. *Wirtschaftsinformatik*, 1177-1190.

Sinha, S. (2017). IoT and Make in India: Exploring new horizons for sustainable Entrepreneurship Development in India. *Circulation in Computer Science*, 14-17.

Siniscalco, M. T., & Auriat, N. (2005). Questionnaire design. *Quantitative Research Methods in Educational Planning, 1-84*.

Smith, G. (2008). Does gender influence online survey participation?: A record-linkage analysis of university faculty online survey response behavior. 1-21.

Soiferman, K. (2010). Compare and Contrast Inductive and Deductive Research Approaches. *Reading Research Quarterly*, 1-23. Retrieved from http://files.eric.ed.gov/fulltext/ED542066.pdf

Stajkovic, A., & Luthans, F. (1998). Social cognitive theory and self-efficacy: going beyond traditional motivational and behavioral approaches. *Organisational Dynamics, 26*, 62-74.

Statista (2019a). Retail IoT spending in South Africa from 2013 to 2018 (in million U.S. dollars). Retrieved from: https://www.statista.com/statistics/486117/retail-iot-spending-in-south-africa/

Statista (2019b). Digital population in South Africa as of January 2019 (in millions). Retrieved from: https://www.statista.com/statistics/685134/south-africa-digital-population/

Statista (2020). Distribution of Social Media Users in South Africa. Retrieved from: https://www.statista.com/statistics/1100988/age-distribution-of-social-media-users-south-africa/

Steijn, W., & Vedder, A. (2015). Privacy concerns, dead or misunderstood? The perceptions of privacy amongst the young and old. *The International Journal of Government & Democracy in the Information Age, 20*, 299-311.

Sutanto, J., Palme, E., Tan, C. H., & Phang, C. W. (2013). Addressing the Personalization-Privacy Paradox: An Empirical Assessment from a Field Experiment on Smartphone Users. *Mis Quarterly, 37*(4), 1141-1164.

Taddei, S., & Contena, B. (2013). Privacy, trust and control: Which relationships with online self-disclosure?. *Computers in Human Behavior, 29*(3), 821-826.

Taddicken, M. (2014). The 'privacy paradox'in the social web: The impact of privacy concerns, individual characteristics, and the perceived social relevance on different forms of self-disclosure. *Journal of Computer-Mediated Communication, 19*(2), 248-273.

Thierer, A. (2013). The pursuit of privacy in a world where information control is failing. *Harv. JL & Pub. Pol'y, 36*, 409-454.

Thomas, D. R. (2006). A general inductive approach for analyzing qualitative evaluation data. *American journal of evaluation, 27*(2), 237-246.

Trepte, S., Reinecke, L., Ellison, N. B., Quiring, O., Yao, M. Z., & Ziegele, M. (2017). A Cross-Cultural Perspective on the Privacy Calculus. *Social Media+ Society*, *3*(1), 1-13.

Turner, A. (2003). *Sampling Frames and Master Samples.* Retrieved from United Nations Secretariat: https://unstats.un.org/Unsd/demographic/meetings/egm/Sampling_1203/docs/no_3.pdf

Van Vuuren, I. E. (2016). IT Security Trust Model-Securing the Human Perimeter. *International Journal of Social Science and Humanity*, *6*(11), 852-858.

Vitak, J., Liao, Y., Kumar, P., Zimmer, M., & Kritikos, K. (2018). Privacy Attitudes and Data Valuation Among Fitness Tracker Users. In *International Conference on Information*, 229-239.

von Entreß-Fürsteneck, M., Buchwald, A., & Urbach, N. (2019). Will I or will I not? Explaining the willingness to disclose personal self-tracking data to a health insurance company. In *Proceedings of the 52nd Hawaii International Conference on System Sciences*. 1351 – 1361.

Walsham, G. (1995). The emergence of interpretivism in IS research. *Information systems research*, *6*(4), 376-394.

Wang, T., Duong, T. D., & Chen, C. C. (2016). Intention to disclose personal information via mobile applications: A privacy calculus perspective. *International Journal of Information Management*, *36*(4), 531-542.

Wang, Y., Meister, D. B., & Gray, P. H. (2013). Social influence and knowledge management systems use: Evidence from panel data. *Mis Quarterly*, *37*(1), 299-313.

Weber, R. H. (2015). The digital future–A challenge for privacy?. *Computer Law & Security Review*, *31*(2), 234-242.

Wei, J. (2016). DDoS on internet of things—a big alarm for the future. 1-10.

Whitman, M., & Mattord, H. (2013). Management of Information Security. United States of America, USA: Cengage Learning. Retrieved From: https://books.google.co.za/books?hl=en&lr=&id=dz3TCQAAQBAJ&oi=fnd&pg=PP1&ots=AQnV0kqnLC&sig=Jhf27DoCE3Rb_RtXDzYq9UPqYw4#v=onepage&q&f=false

Williams, M. (2018). *Exploring the influence of privacy awareness on the Privacy Paradox on smartwatches* (Doctoral book, University of Oxford). 1-395.

Williams, M., Nurse, J. R., & Creese, S. (2016). The perfect storm: The privacy paradox and the Internet-of-Things. In *Availability, Reliability and Security (ARES), 2016 11th International Conference,* 644-652.

Williams, M., Nurse, J. R., & Creese, S. (2017). " Privacy is the boring bit": User perceptions and behaviour in the Internet– of– Things. *In the Proceedings of the 15th International Conference on Privacy, Security and Trust*, 1-10.

Williams, R., McMahon, E., Samtani, S., Patton, M., & Chen, H. (2017, July). Identifying vulnerabilities of consumer Internet of Things (IoT) devices: A scalable approach. In *2017 IEEE International Conference on Intelligence and Security Informatics (ISI)* (pp. 179-181).

Witti, M., & Konstantas, D. (2019). IOT and Security-Privacy Concerns: A Systematic Mapping Study. 25-33.

Wu, H., Zhang, H., Cui, L., & Wang, X. (2018). A Heuristic Model for Supporting Users' Decision-Making in Privacy Disclosure for Recommendation. *Security and Communication Networks, 2018*. 1-13.

Xu, H., Dinev, T., Smith, J., & Hart, P. (2011). Information privacy concerns: Linking individual perceptions with institutional privacy assurances. Journal of the Association for Information Systems, 12(12), 798-824.

Xu, H., Luo, X. R., Carroll, J. M., & Rosson, M. B. (2011). The personalization privacy paradox: An exploratory study of decision making process for location-aware marketing. *Decision support systems*, *51*(1), 42-52.

Xu, H., Teo, H. H., Tan, B. C., & Agarwal, R. (2012). Research note—effects of individual self-protection, industry self-regulation, and government regulation on privacy concerns: A study of location-based services. *Information Systems Research*, *23*(4), 1342-1363.

Yang, H., Yu, J., Zo, H., & Choi, M. (2016). User acceptance of wearable devices: An extended perspective of perceived value. *Telematics and Informatics*, *33*(2), 256-269.

Zafeiropoulou, A. M., Millard, D. E., Webber, C., & O'Hara, K. (2013). Unpicking the privacy paradox: can structuration theory help to explain location-based privacy decisions?. In *Proceedings of the 5th Annual ACM Web Science Conference* (pp. 463-472).

Zheng, S., Chetty, M., & Feamster, N. (2018). User Perceptions of Privacy in Smart Homes. 1-9.

Zhou, J., Cao, Z., Dong, X., & Vasilakos, A. V. (2017). Security and Privacy for Cloud-Based IoT: Challenges. *IEEE Communications Magazine*, *55*(1), 26-33.

Zhou, T. (2011). Understanding online community user participation: a social influence perspective. *Internet research*, *21*(1), 67-81.

Zhou, T., & Li, H. (2014). Understanding mobile SNS continuance usage in China from the perspectives of social influence and privacy concern. *Computers in Human Behavior*, *37*, 283-289.

7. Appendices

7.1. Appendix A: Ethics Approval

07/06/2018

Ms Natheer Davids
Department Of Information System
University of Cape Town

REF: REC 2018/005/039

Dear Natheer Davids,

The Privacy Paradox: Factors Influencing Information Disclosure in the use of the Internet of Things (IoT), within South Africa

We are pleased to inform you that your ethics application has been approved. Unless otherwise specified this ethical clearance is valid for 1 year and may be renewed upon application.

 Please be aware that you need to notify the Ethics Committee immediately should any aspect of your study regarding the engagement with participants as approved in this application, change. This may include aspects such as changes to the research design, questionnaires, or choice of participants. The ongoing ethical conduct throughout the duration of the study remains the responsibility of the principal investigator.

We wish you well for your research.

Modie Sempu
Administrative   Assistant
University of Cape Town
Commerce Faculty Office
Room 2.26 | Leslie Commerce Building

Office Telephone: +27 (0)21 650 2695/4375
Office Fax: +27 (0)21 650 4369
E-mail: modie.sempu@uct.ac.za
Website: www.commerce.uct.ac.za<http://www.commerce.uct.ac.za/

	RESEARCH ACCESS TO STUDENTS	**DSA 100**

NOTES

1. This form must be **FULLY** completed by all applicants who want to access UCT students for the purpose of research or surveys.
2. Return the fully completed **(a) DSA 100** application form **by email**, in **the same word format**, together with **your: (b) research proposal inclusive of your survey, (c)** copy of your ethics approval letter / proof **(d) informed consent letter** to: Moonira.Khan@uct.ac.za. You application will be attended to by the Executive Director, Department of Student Affairs (DSA), UCT.
3. The turnaround time for a reply is **approximately 10 working days**.
4. NB: It is the responsibility of the researcher/s to apply for and to obtain **ethics approval and to comply with amendments that may be requested**; as well as **to obtain** approval to access UCT staff and/or UCT students, from the following, at UCT, respectively:
   (a) **Ethics**: Chairperson, Faculty Research Ethics Committee' (FREC) for ethics approval, (b) **Staff access**: Executive Director: HR for approval to access UCT staff, and (c) **Student access**: Executive Director: Student Affairs for approval to access UCT students.
5. **Note**: UCT Senate Research Protocols requires compliance to the above, **even if prior approval has been obtained from any other institution/agency**. UCT's research protocol requirements applies to *all* persons, institutions and agencies from UCT and external to UCT who want to conduct research on human subjects for academic, marketing or service related reasons at UCT.
6. Should approval be granted to access UCT students for this research study, such approval is effective for a period of one year from the date of approval (as stated in Section D of this form), and the approval expires automatically on the last day.
7. The approving authority reserves the right to revoke an approval based on reasonable grounds and/or new information.

SECTION A: RESEARCH APPLICANT/S DETAILS

Position	Staff / Student No	Title and Name	Contact Details (Email / Cell / land line)
A.1 Student Number	DVDNAT008	Mr Natheer Davids	DVDNAT008@myuct.ac.za / 0832512091
A.2 Academic / PASS Staff No.			
A.3 Visitor/ Researcher ID No.			
A.4 University at which a student or employee	University of Cape Town	Address if *not* UCT:	
A.5 Faculty/ Department/School	Faculty of Commerce/Department of Information Systems		
A.6 APPLICANTS DETAILS If different from above	Title and Name	Tel.	Email

SECTION B: RESEARCHER/S SUPERVISOR/S DETAILS

Position	Title and Name	Tel.	Email
B.1 Supervisor	Assoc Prof Kevin Johnston	+27 (21) 650-2266	kevin.johnston@uct.ac.za
B.2 Co-Supervisor/s			

SECTION C: APPLICANT'S RESEARCH STUDY FIELD AND APPROVAL STATUS

C.1 Degree – if applicable	Master of Commerce (MCom): Specialising in Information Systems
C.2 Research Project Title	The Privacy Paradox: Factors Influencing Information Disclosure in the use of the Internet of Things (IoT), within South Africa
C.3 Research Proposal	Attached: Yes ■ No ☐
C.4 Target population	UCT students
C.5 Lead Researcher details	If different from applicant:
C6. Will use research assistant/s	Yes ☐ No ■ If yes- provide a list of names, contact details :
C.7 Research Methodology and Informed consent	Research methodology: Quantitative and qualitative online questionnaire, mixed method, cross sectional study. Informed consent: Yes, advised before commencement of questionnaire
C.8 Ethics clearance status from UCT's Faculty Ethics in Research Committee /Chair (EiRC)	Approved by the UCT EiRC: Yes ■ With amendments: Yes ☐ No ■ (a) Attach copy of your UCT ethics approval. Attached: Yes ■ No ☐ (b) State date/Ref. No/Faculty of your UCT ethics approval: 07/06/2018 Ref./Faculty: REC 2018/005/039

SECTION D: APPLICANT/S APPROVAL STATUS FOR ACCESS TO STUDENTS FOR RESEARCH PURPOSE
(To be completed by the UCT - ED, DSA or Nominee)

D.1 APPROVAL STATUS	Approved / With Terms / Not	* Conditional approval with terms	Applicant/s Ref. No.:
	(i) Approved ■ (ii) With terms (iii) Not approved	a) Access to students for this research study must only be undertaken *after* written ethics approval has been obtained. b) In event any ethics conditions are attached, these must be complied with *before* access to students.	DVDNAT008 / Mr Natheer Davids

D.2 APPROVED BY:	Designation	Name	Signature	Date of Approval
	Executive Director Department of Student Affairs	Dr Moonira Khan	*[signature]*	27 June 2018

B

Department of Information Systems

<u>Request to conduct research and interview participation consent form</u>

Dear Sir/Madam,

In terms of the requirements for completing a Master of Commerce Degree in Information Systems at the University of Cape Town a research study is required.

The researcher, in this case Natheer Davids, has chosen to conduct a study entitled "The Privacy Paradox: Factors Influencing Information Disclosure in the use of the Internet of Things (IoT), within South Africa". The objective of the research is to explain the potential dichotomy between information sharing and privacy (referred to as the Privacy Paradox), through factors that influence personal information disclosure in the use of IoT.

You are invited to partake in in an anonymous questionnaire. Your participation in this research is voluntary. All information will be treated in a confidential manner and used exclusively for the purpose of this study. No individual names will be recorded or published. You will not be requested to supply any identifiable information, ensuring anonymity of your responses.

By participating in the questionnaire, you are subsequently giving consent for the researcher to analyse your answers. You can choose to withdraw from the research at any time for whatever reason, in accordance with ethical research requirements. The findings of this research will be compiled into a report and presented to the University of Cape Town for academic purposes.

The data collection method will be an online questionnaire. The questionnaire will be conducted online and will last approximately 10-15 minutes. This research has been approved by the Commerce Faculty Ethics in Research Committee.

Should you have any questions regarding this research, please feel free to contact me on 0832512091 or email: DVDNAT008@myuct.ac.za

Your participation in this study would be greatly appreciated but is entirely voluntary.

Sincerely,

Natheer Davids

Researcher \ M.Com Student, (UCT)
Department of Information Systems
University of Cape Town
Email: DVDNAT008@myuct.ac.za

Associate Professor Kevin Johnston

Research Supervisor
Department of Information Systems
University of Cape Town
Email: kevin.johnston@uct.ac.za

Section 1: Demographics and general understanding of the research topic

1. Your current age:

Below 18 ☐   18-29 ☐   30-39 ☐   40-49 ☐   50-59 ☐   Above 60 ☐

2. What gender do you currently identify yourself as?

Male ☐   Female ☐   Other ☐   Prefer not to answer ☐

3. Are you currently living in South Africa?

Yes ☐   No ☐

4. What is your current highest educational qualification?

No Schooling Completed	☐
High School Certificate	☐
Vocational Certificate	☐
Diploma	☐
University Undergraduate Degree	☐
University Postgraduate Degree	☐

5. Have you heard of the term "Internet of Things (IoT)", prior to this study?

Yes ☐   No ☐

6. IoT consist of everyday devices such as smartphones, smartphone applications (such as Snapscan etc.), smart TVs, fitness watches, laptops and tablets etc. with that in mind, how often do you use IoT devices and applications?

A great deal	A lot	A moderate amount	A little	Not at all
1	2	3	4	5

7. In what instance are you most likely to use IoT devices?

Work-related ☐   Leisure ☐   Fitness ☐   Other ☐

8. Do you know that IoT devices quietly and continuously accumulate your personal data (i.e. location data and health data)?

Yes ☐   No ☐

Section 2: Information sensitivity

	Hypotheses: H1					
		Very Willing	Probably will	Neutral	Willing Probably will not	Definitely will not
	Information Sensitivity					
1	My real first name	1	2	3	4	5
2	My real last name	1	2	3	4	5
3	My real date of birth	1	2	3	4	5
4	My real e-mail address	1	2	3	4	5
5	My Identification (ID) number	1	2	3	4	5
6	My real home address	1	2	3	4	5
7	My real banking details	1	2	3	4	5
8	My real medical history	1	2	3	4	5
9	My current location	1	2	3	4	5
10	I would allow my device to track my health and movement even when I am not actively using it in that moment	1	2	3	4	5

Section 3: Privacy Concern

	Hypotheses: H3					
		Strongly Agree	Somewhat agree	Neither agree nor disagree	Somewhat disagree	Strongly disagree
	Privacy Concern					
1	I consider myself to be someone that values their privacy	1	2	3	4	5
2	I am highly concerned about the way others handle my personal information	1	2	3	4	5
3	In general, personal privacy is a very important subject on my mind.	1	2	3	4	5
4	I am concerned about threats to my personal privacy	1	2	3	4	5
5	To me, it is an important thing to keep my privacy intact from others.	1	2	3	4	5

	Hypotheses: H6 & H7					
		Strongly Agree	Somewhat agree	Neither agree nor disagree	Somewhat disagree	Strongly disagree
	Privacy Knowledge					
1	I have an adequate level of knowledge about privacy settings of IoT devices and applications that I use, to protect myself against potential privacy loss?	1	2	3	4	5
2	I have an adequate level of knowledge about the way manufacturers of my IoT devices and applications store and use my personal information? (i.e. Apple, Samsung, Fitbit etc.)	1	2	3	4	5
3	Overall, I know the potential risks involved and possible negative consequences involved in using IoT devices and applications.	1	2	3	4	5

	Hypotheses: H5					
		Strongly Agree	Somewhat agree	Neither agree nor disagree	Somewhat disagree	Strongly disagree
	Social Influence					
1	Most of my friends/family use IoT devices	1	2	3	4	5
2	My friends/family actively disclose their personal information on smartphone applications (i.e. social media, health applications etc.)	1	2	3	4	5
3	I am more likely to disclose my personal information over a platform or device if my friends/family/colleagues are doing so	1	2	3	4	5
4	I am more likely to use a particular device or application, if my friends/family/colleagues are using it as well	1	2	3	4	5
5	By sharing too much personal information. I could run into problems with my friends/family.	1	2	3	4	5

Section 6: Self-Withdrawal

	Hypotheses: H8 & H9					
		Strongly Agree	Somewh at agree	Neither agree nor disagree	Some what disagr ee	Strongly disagree
	Self-withdrawal					
1	I will adopt self-withdrawal behaviours (i.e. removing myself off a social media application, or stop using an IoT device), if potential risks outweigh potential benefits in the use of IoT devices and applications	1	2	3	4	5
2	If my personal information was stolen or compromised through an application or device, I would adopt self-withdrawal behaviour and stop divulging my personal information over applications and devices.	1	2	3	4	5
3	Generally, I would withdraw myself from a situation which I believe could be detrimental to my privacy	1	2	3	4	5

Section 7: Perceived Benefits

	Hypotheses: H4					
	Perceived Benefits	Strongly Agree	Somewhat agree	Neither agree nor disagree	Some what disagr ee	Strongly disagree
1	I think potential benefits gained from the use of IoT devices and applications can offset the risks of my information disclosure.	1	2	3	4	5
2	Overall, I feel that using IoT devices and applications is beneficial	1	2	3	4	5
	Personalised Services					
1	IoT devices and applications can provide me with more relevant promotional information tailored to my preferences or personal interests (i.e. shopping related content)	1	2	3	4	5
2	IoT devices and applications reduce my searching time to find promotional information that I need (i.e. smartphones, social media etc.)	1	2	3	4	5
	Self-Presentation					
1	I present myself in a realistic manner when disclosing personal information using IoT devices and applications (i.e. real weight on health apps etc.)	1	2	3	4	5
2	I believe that by using a particular IoT device, I can present myself in a desired manner (i.e. using an Apple Watch makes me look affluent	1	2	3	4	5

	or using a smart watch makes me look sporty etc.)					
	Enjoyment					
1	I spend enjoyable and relaxing time using IoT devices and applications	1	2	3	4	5
2	I find IoT devices and applications entertaining	1	2	3	4	5
3	When I am bored, I often use IoT devices and applications	1	2	3	4	5

Section 8: Perceived Risks

	Hypotheses: H3					
	Perceived Risks	Strongly Agree	Somewhat agree	Neither agree nor disagree	Somewhat disagree	Strongly disagree
1	There is a lot of uncertainty associated with providing my personal information in the use of IoT devices and applications	1	2	3	4	5
2	There is a high possibility for loss/misuse of my personal information, if I use IoT devices and applications	1	2	3	4	5
3	Providing my private information when using IoT devices and applications, could bring about unexpected problems	1	2	3	4	5

Section 9: Intentions to disclose

	Intentions to disclose (Dependent Variable)					
		Strongly Agree	Somewhat agree	Neither agree nor disagree	Somewhat disagree	Strongly disagree
	Intentions to disclose personal information in the use of IoT	1	2	3	4	5
1	I am likely to disclose my personal information when using IoT devices and applications	1	2	3	4	5
2	I am willing to disclose my personal information when using IoT devices and applications, to gain benefits, regardless of the associated risks that may be involved	1	2	3	4	5

	Mean	Standard Deviation
InfoSen_1	2,04	0,95
InfoSen_2	2,29	0,99
InfoSen_3	2,36	1,06
InfoSen_4	2,36	1,03
InfoSen_5	3,93	1,07
InfoSen_6	3,98	1,05
InfoSen_7	4,38	0,90
InfoSen_8	3,78	1,16
InfoSen_9	3,72	1,11
InfoSen_10	2,90	1,20
PrivCon_1	1,44	0,62
PrivCon_2	1,66	0,83
PrivCon_3	1,62	0,81
PrivCon_4	1,50	0,70
PrivKnow_1	2,30	1,05
PrivKnow_2	2,82	1,19
PrivKnow_3	2,29	1,08
SocInf_1	1,30	0,58
SocInf_2	2,28	0,91
SocInf_3	2,88	1,26
SocInf_4	2,32	1,11
SocInf_5	2,44	1,17
SelfWith_1	1,78	0,92
SelfWith_2	1,50	0,85
SelfWith_3	1,46	0,70
PerBen_1	2,48	1,03
PerBen_2	1,91	0,73
PerBen (PS)_3	1,93	0,94
PerBen (PS)_4	2,03	0,94
PerBen (SP)_5	1,85	0,87
PerBen (SP)_6	2,89	1,28
PerBen (EN)_7	1,71	0,79
PerBen (EN)_8	1,66	0,73
PerBen (EN)_9	1,55	0,85
PerRisk_1	1,81	0,77
PerRisk_2	1,99	0,91
PerRisk_3	1,91	0,84
IntDis_1	2,82	1,14
IntDis_2	3,34	1,18

7.6. Appendix F: Initial Model's Outer Loadings

Variable	Outer Loading	Outer Loading Value
Information Sensitivity	InfoSen_1	0,58
	InfoSen_2	0,60
	InfoSen_3	0,74
	InfoSen_4	0,61
	InfoSen_5	0,75
	InfoSen_6	0,63
	InfoSen_7	0,60
	InfoSen_8	0,52
	InfoSen_9	0,50
	InfoSen_10	0,44
Privacy Concern	PrivCon_1	0,61
	PrivCon_2	0,76
	PrivCon_3	0,80
	PrivCon_4	0,71
Perceived Risk	PerRisk_1	0,69
	PerRisk_2	0,75
	PerRisk_3	0,85
Perceived Benefit	PerBen_1	0,47
	PerBen_2	0,46
	PerBen(PS)_3	0,56
	PerBen(PS)_4	0,50
	PerBen(SP)_5	0,38
	PerBen(SP)_6	0,66
	PerBen(EN)_7	0,51
	PerBen(EN)_8	0,60
	PerBen(EN)_9	0,49
Social influence	SocInf_1	0,30
	SocInf_2	0,44
	SocInf_3	0,71
	SocInf_4	0,62
	SocInf_5	0,03

Self-Withdrawal	SelfWith_1	0,67
	SelfWith_2	0,65
	SelfWith_3	0,81
Privacy Knowledge	PrivKnow_1	1,02
	PrivKnow_2	0,68
	PrivKnow_3	0,56
Intention to Disclose	IntDis_1	0,77
	IntDis_2	0,71

7.7. Appendix G: Re-evaluated Model's Outer Loadings

Variable	Outer Loading	Outer Loading Value
Information Sensitivity	InfoSen_1	0,59
	InfoSen_2	0,59
	InfoSen_3	0,74
	InfoSen_4	0,57
	InfoSen_5	0,80
	InfoSen_6	0,70
	InfoSen_7	0,64
	InfoSen_8	0,55
	InfoSen_9	0,50
Privacy Concern	PrivCon_1	0,61
	PrivCon_2	0,76
	PrivCon_3	0,80
	PrivCon_4	0,70
Perceived Risk	PerRisk_1	0,68
	PerRisk_2	0,76
	PerRisk_3	0,85
Perceived Benefit	PerBen_1	0,68
	PerBen(EN)_7	0,63
	PerBen(EN)_8	0,70
	PerBen(EN)_9	0,55
Social influence	SocInf_3	0,84
	SocInf_4	0,72

Self-Withdrawal	SelfWith_1	0,67
	SelfWith_2	0,62
	SelfWith_3	0,83
Privacy Knowledge	PrivKnow_1	1,04
	PrivKnow_2	0,65
	PrivKnow_3	0,56
Intention to Disclose	IntDis_1	0,77
	IntDis_2	0,71